Praise for *The Tapping Solution to Create Lasting Change*

"The Tapping Solution to Create Lasting Change gets right down to the heart of what it takes to change and have a better, healthier, and more love-filled life. It addresses the most persistent blocks to change that all of us have. And then tells us exactly how to gently and easily dissolve them. Here are the tools that literally tap into the very essence of what we all need to do to be open to receiving our highest and best lives."

— Christiane Northrup, M.D., *New York Times* best-selling author of
Goddesses Never Age and *Dodging Energy Vampires*

"If you're tired of feeling stuck and unable to make the changes you know you want to make, let this book become your new best friend. Jessica Ortner is an experienced 'changemaker' with wisdom beyond her years. She's created a smart program that will show you exactly how to use powerful Tapping techniques to quickly and easily move forward in your life. If you're ready to face your fear, overcome procrastination, and start living life with more joy and ease, use this book and tap your way to transformation now!"

— Cheryl Richardson, *New York Times* best-selling author of
The Art of Extreme Self-Care

"If you have big dreams but have struggled with procrastination and self-doubt, this book is a must. I've used Tapping in my own life and have been amazed by the results. Jessica Ortner is the perfect guide to help you get unstuck and find your flow."

— Kris Carr, *New York Times* best-selling author of *Crazy Sexy Kitchen* and *Crazy Sexy Juice*

"Within *The Tapping Solution to Create Lasting Change*, you're about to find a dear friend and transformational partner in Jessica Ortner. I can assure you she is as warm and authentic in person as she is in print, and as you relish her wisdom and relate to the stories of her own come-from-behind manifestations, you'll thank the day your paths crossed. This is a stellar book by an amazing woman who will help untold people."

— Mike Dooley, *New York Times* best-selling author of
Infinite Possibilities and *Playing the Matrix*

"Do you often feel like you get in your own way, and changing your life just seems too hard? If so, open this book to learn how to break through common blocks like doubt and overwhelm and claim your best life now. Happiness and well-being will be a vital foundation of your everyday life. You deserve it! You will love this book. Tapping is an incredible tool and Jessica is a masterful teacher. Highly recommended."

— Colette Baron-Reid, spiritual teacher and best-selling author of
The Map and *Uncharted*

"*The Tapping Solution to Create Lasting Change* is unflinchingly honest, practical, humorous, and real. Jessica expertly illustrates the ways we can flow through change in our lives to find the clarity and the simplicity we crave to move forward. A simply wonderful read."

— Dr. Mike Dow, *New York Times* best-selling author of *The Brain Fog Fix* and *Heal Your Drained Brain*

The

Tapping
Solution

TO

Create Lasting
Change

Also by Jessica Ortner

The Tapping Solution for Weight Loss & Body Confidence

The above is available at your local bookstore,
or may be ordered by visiting:

Hay House USA: www.hayhouse.com®
Hay House Australia: www.hayhouse.com.au
Hay House UK: www.hayhouse.co.uk
Hay House India: www.hayhouse.co.in

ᕁ

The Tapping Solution

TO

Create Lasting Change

A Guide to Get Unstuck *and* Find Your Flow

JESSICA ORTNER

HAY HOUSE, INC.

Carlsbad, California • New York City
London • Sydney • New Delhi

Published in the United States by: Hay House, Inc.: www.hayhouse.com® • *Published in Australia by:* Hay House Australia Pty. Ltd.: www.hayhouse.com.au • *Published in the United Kingdom by:* Hay House UK, Ltd.: www.hayhouse.co.uk • *Published in India by:* Hay House Publishers India: www.hayhouse.co.in

Cover design: Julie Rosenberger • *Interior design:* Nick C. Welch
Interior illustrations: Deanna Maree, www.deannamaree.studio
Tapping points diagram and "pattern of panic" graphic: Courtesy of The Tapping Solution
Indexer: Jay Kreider

Library of Congress Cataloging-in-Publication Data

Names: Ortner, Jessica, 1985- author.
Title: The tapping solution to create lasting change : a guide to get unstuck
   and find your flow / Jessica Ortner.
Description: Carlsbad, California : Hay House Inc., 2018.
Identifiers: LCCN 2018016398 | ISBN 9781401953683 (hardback)
Subjects: LCSH: Emotional Freedom Techniques. | Women--Health and hygiene. |
   Mind and body therapies. | Stress management. | Self-care, Health. |
   BISAC: SELF-HELP / Personal Growth / Happiness. | SELF-HELP / Motivational
   & Inspirational.
Classification: LCC RC489.E45 O76 2018 | DDC 616.89/1--dc23 LC record available at https://lccn.
loc.gov/2018016398

Hardcover ISBN: 978-1-4019-5368-3
E-book ISBN: 978-1-4019-5369-0
Audiobook ISBN: 978-1-4019-5390-4

10 9 8 7 6 5 4 3 2 1

1st edition, September 2018

Printed in the United States of America

To my husband, Lucas,
thank you for always leading me
out of my head and into my heart.

Dear reader,

I'm so happy and honored that you are here.
I've made some special resources available to
support you on your journey. You can find
exclusive tapping meditation audios and much
more here.

www.thetappingsolution.com/lastingchange

CONTENTS

INTRODUCTION

As soon as I answered my phone, I felt a mixture of relief and panic. My heart felt lighter just imagining expressing my feelings, but my brain had a different plan. It wanted me to pretend that I was fine, to say that things were busy but good.

Admittedly, from the outside my life did look good. A few weeks before, my first book, *The Tapping Solution for Weight Loss & Body Confidence*, had become a *New York Times* bestseller. Since the book's release, I'd appeared on television, been interviewed by major magazines and celebrated by followers, friends, and family. Privately, though, I'd been struggling, overwhelmed by the attention and anxious that I couldn't meet what felt like mounting expectations.

As I began speaking into my phone that day, I wasn't sure how much I should say . . . and not say. Thankfully, it was Cheryl Richardson on the other end of the line. In addition to being a self-care expert and a repeat *New York Times* best-selling author herself, she is one of the most compassionate, caring people I've ever known.

Cheryl's soothing, empathetic tone quickly paved the way for an authentic, heart-centered exchange. Before long the floodgates of my emotions opened, and I voiced the painful truths I'd been working hard to hide.

Of course I was (and still am!) overjoyed about becoming a best-selling author. It was an honor and a thrill, and incredible validation that years of hard work were having a positive impact. For weeks, though, I'd been playing the part of the confident first-time author, while inside I felt increasingly unsure of myself.

The worst part was that I'd been so busy speaking and doing interviews about the power of Tapping that I had unintentionally let my own practice slip. Distracted by my demanding schedule, I'd been inconsistent with the practice that I knew kept me balanced and feeling my best. It felt like a sure sign that I was a phony; I knew better, yet I wasn't following through.

As I spoke, my tears flowed easily and abundantly. Then, as only she can do, Cheryl decoded my entire experience. In the most motherly, generous voice, she said, "Jess, when you are scared because of something new, you're not adult Jessica. You're not the resourceful adult who knows how to tap. You're this little girl who is really scared. And that little girl doesn't know how to tap. That scared part of you deserves your own compassion first and foremost."

As soon as Cheryl said those words, I exhaled. She had captured my experience so perfectly that my relief was physical as well as emotional. I could suddenly see that I'd been suppressing the mature, resourceful adult I am. Up until that moment, my fear had temporarily caused me to resort to a younger version of myself.

Have you ever done that? It's what we often do when we're faced with new circumstances. We expect ourselves to be resourceful and productive when, on a deeper level, we're overwhelmed by a primal fear of the unknown.

Truthfully, that fear had snuck back into my life. During the months surrounding my book launch, I'd told myself repeatedly that I'd be fine once the book launch was over. It was just my schedule, the constant demands. The problem, I kept telling myself, was my *external* circumstances. Ironically, during the many months prior to the launch, which I'd spent writing the book, my stress had been around how my book would be received. I wanted, really wanted, the book to be a bestseller. When my book did hit the bestsellers list, my primitive brain found new reasons to freak out.

That's what the primitive brain does. It constantly scans your internal and external surroundings to locate new threats and unforeseen dangers. It doesn't kick back and relax once you've reached a goal. Instead it prods and pokes at your successes (and everything else in your life) to find the shadow side. Once it finds those dark spots, it rushes in to reveal those findings. That's how it keeps you continuously cycling through what I call the *pattern of panic*. (For a visual reference, you can check out a diagram of the pattern of panic on page 25.)

The primitive brain's tireless search for danger, even in positive developments like reaching a major milestone, is why focusing on external circumstances—love, money, success, and more—as ways to "fix" our lives never delivers the peace of mind and flow we hope for.

Once Cheryl had given me the space that day to replace my self-judgment with compassion, we spent time tapping together on the phone, processing and releasing everything I'd been feeling. Afterward I felt lighter, like a dense weight had been lifted off of me. From that day forward, I resumed my regular Tapping meditation practice, and made sure to take time each day to connect with my inner self—this time *without* the panic.

Still, though, I had questions. I reached out to friends and colleagues who are also authors. Each of them reassured me that what I was feeling was part of the process. As the weeks turned into months, I found myself repeatedly asking questions like:

Why *do* we fear the unknown so intensely that we're willing to shy away from our deepest desires and settle for playing small?

Why *do* we get enthused when we first start something, only to burn out the moment things feel challenging?

Why *does* getting what we want sometimes feel just as scary as not getting what we want? And why, even with new outcomes we desire, do we often struggle to sustain them and instead slip back into old, self-sabotaging patterns?

Eventually it became clear that I was exploring our relationship with the one unavoidable constant in life:

Change.

It's a word that evokes many different, often conflicting emotions—fear, excitement, dread, desire, anxiety, longing, frustration—and that's the short list! Overwhelmed by our emotions around change, we often react in one of two ways.

We may judge ourselves for feeling unease around change and decide that our initial fear must mean that we aren't good enough or ready enough to handle the change we're facing. In other words, we turn the challenging emotions we experience around change into a problem. We let our discomfort around change dictate our actions and limit our options.

At other times when we're faced with change, we rely on willpower and pushing to move through our discomfort. This strategy usually works for a while, and may even yield impressive results. Eventually, though, we become exhausted or get distracted and give up.

However we react to change, whether it's change that seems beyond our control or change that we consciously create, we become so overwhelmed by the unknown inherent in change that on some level we freeze. We get stuck in our old limiting responses to change. When that happens, we're likely to sabotage even change we desire and set out to create. That's the primitive brain at work, trying to protect us from the intense discomfort we feel around the uncertainty of change.

As I continued to explore my deeper experience, I began to realize that our relationship with change doesn't need to be fixed; it needs to be understood. With a fuller understanding of why we react to change in certain ways, we can more easily flow through it instead of becoming so overwhelmed that we get stuck.

Much to my surprise, in the months following that phone call with Cheryl, I began to seek out more major changes in my life—pursuing new places to live, as well as new creative, professional, and personal experiences. Through those often surprising, sometimes challenging adventures, I continued my deep dive into the change process, allowing myself to move through the fear, anxiety, and other challenging emotions it evokes. I noticed self-sabotaging patterns that can trip us up, and figured out how to navigate the rough patches instead of getting stuck in them.

Through months, then years, of trial and error, I discovered what it looks and feels like to flow through change. I figured out how to create positive, lasting change in ways that feel authentic, and ultimately empowering as well.

What I discovered in the end is both surprising and not surprising at all— that there's profound beauty and joy in change, even when it doesn't initially feel that way. When we can flow through change without resistance or judgment and let ourselves feel the full scope of our emotions, we can have an entirely new experience around change. Steeped in our trust and faith in life, we can navigate the unknown that's inherent in change with new energy, inspiration, and openheartedness. We can create movement in our lives in ways that feel good, even when circumstances don't reflect our previous hopes and expectations.

That's the process I guide you through in this book. Rather than judging ourselves for the discomfort that naturally arises around change, we can acknowledge it and flow through it with greater ease and self-acceptance.

Using this process, you will gain greater clarity and insight as you begin to create change. While the experience may not always feel entirely comfortable, your discomfort around change will also become less of an obstacle. Through that larger journey, you will rediscover your flow, and feel more joy in the ordinary and extraordinary everyday experiences you inevitably have as you create lasting and empowering change.

One of several reasons this process is so powerful is its use of Tapping, which allows you to more easily move through your emotions. Most of us know how challenging it is to let go of big emotions like fear, anxiety, anger, and more. We tell ourselves we don't need to be afraid, but on a deeper level, we still are. We reason that it's time to release our anger, yet it's still there, in the body and mind, ready to be triggered when we least expect it.

The truth is, I can give you an inspirational quote about why it's your time to realize your deeper desires and create lasting change. I can give you strategies, insights, even shortcuts for moving forward. None of this will matter if you don't address your emotions on a body-mind level.

Using Tapping, you can reassure the mind-body that you are safe, creating the lasting change you desire. With Tapping you can make peace with the fact that change, including manifesting your desires, is unnerving. Instead of judging your emotions, you can feel and release them and create movement that supports your growth and expansion, both internally and externally.

It has been an honor and privilege to share this process with hundreds of clients, many of whom have amazed themselves by moving through many different kinds of change feeling more energized and empowered than they have in a long time. They, like I, discovered how to create change, make it stick, and then manifest better outcomes than they'd previously dared to envision. None of those clients could claim idyllic external circumstances, yet they, like me, were able to create lasting changes that felt fulfilling and profoundly authentic to who they are and what they desire.

As you begin this journey, you'll notice that each chapter offers a Tapping Meditation at the end, as well as sample Tapping scripts throughout. Each sample script within the various chapters corresponds to a complete, extended version, which you will find in the Appendix. To support you throughout this journey and beyond, I've also included additional bonus scripts in the Appendix that are not referenced in the book, but will help you to overcome general yet common stumbling blocks I've observed in myself and in clients over the years.

I hope you'll join me, and countless others, in creating the kinds of lasting change that allow you to shine your brightest. I've never been more excited to witness your journey. I've never felt so ready to support and applaud the powerful lasting change you create.

Your time is now, and I'm thrilled to be here, taking this journey right alongside you.

With love,
Jessica Ortner

TAPPING QUICK
START GUIDE

In this section I'll guide you through how to tap, demonstrating how to customize the practice to meet your needs and your experiences. Approach Tapping with a curious and compassionate spirit. If you follow the general guidelines, you can and will experience the relief you desire.

Resetting Your Mind-Body

So how does this "Tapping thing" work?

Tapping on meridian points, which we'll discuss soon, sends a calming signal to the brain, letting your brain know it's safe to relax. When you receive bad news from your boss or you begin to future-trip (worrying about future events), it triggers a part of your brain called the amygdala. When you think of the amygdala, one word should come to mind. Fear. This part of the brain is responsible for triggering the stress response in our bodies, releasing a cocktail of certain stress-related hormones into the bloodstream. Also popularly known as the fight-or-flight response, it is the body's natural reaction to a perceived threat. This is helpful when you're faced with real-life danger but damaging when you want to feel calm and confident during a high-stakes meeting. Tapping on your body while you think about what is causing you stress helps your mind understand that you are not in any physical danger and it is safe to relax.

In a double-blind study conducted by Dawson Church, Ph.D., participants were divided into two groups. One group was led through an hour of a form of Tapping known as Emotional Freedom Technique (EFT), while the other, which was the control group, was given an hour of conventional talk therapy.

The Tapping group showed an average of a 24 percent decrease in levels of the "stress hormone" cortisol, with some experiencing as much as a 50 percent decrease in cortisol.

In contrast the control group, which received conventional talk therapy, showed only a 14 percent drop of cortisol.

Dawson recently published an additional study about the powerful effects of Emotional Freedom Techniques (EFT) on gene expression. This newer study was published in the journal *Energy Psychology*. Dawson summarized these new findings in this way:

> *Levels of gene expression are like the gradations of a light controlled by a dimmer switch; the expression of many genes can be dialed up or down. Stress, hunger, tiredness, mood and many other experiences affect gene expression levels.*
>
> *In this pilot study, investigator Beth Maharaj compared an hour of EFT to an hour of social interaction in 4 subjects. She found that 72 genes were significantly regulated after EFT.*
>
> *The functions of these genes [are] fascinating. Among them were: the suppression of cancer tumors, protection against the sun's ultraviolet radiation, type 2 diabetes insulin resistance, immunity from opportunistic infections, antiviral activity, synaptic connectivity between neurons, creation of both red and white blood cells, enhancement of male fertility, building white matter in the brain, metabolic regulation, neural plasticity, strengthening cell membranes, and reducing oxidative stress.*
>
> *This and other studies suggest that EFT is an epigenetic intervention, regulating the expression of many genes. Just an hour of EFT is doing your body a whole lot of good.*[1]

The incredible results that Tapping has on relieving stress may be explained, at least in part, by its ability to access what are called meridian channels.

Although awareness of these channels dates back to thousands of years of ancient Chinese medicine, it wasn't until the 1960s that these threadlike microscopic anatomical structures were first seen on stereomicroscope and electron microscope images.

Those scans showed tubular structures measuring 30 to 100 micrometers wide running up and down the body. Described in a published paper by a North Korean researcher named Kim Bonghan, they are also referred to as "Bonghan channels." As a reference point, one red blood cell is six to eight micrometers wide, so these structures are tiny!

You can think of meridian channels as a fiber-optic network in the body. They carry a large amount of information, often electrical and often beyond what the nervous system or chemical systems of the body can carry. By accessing these channels while processing emotions and thoughts, as well as physical conditions like pain, Tapping gets to the root cause of stress more quickly than other stress-relief techniques can.

That is a very quick, cursory view on the science and research, but if you want to see some of the many papers published on its effectiveness, go here: www.thetappingsolution.com/science-research.

Now that we've seen some of the science and research, it's time to ask the most important question—what can Tapping do for *you?*

What's Bothering You Now

The journey we'll take in this book will enable you to create lasting change and find your flow, but the optimal starting point with Tapping is not where you intend to go; it's where you are now—mentally, emotionally, even physically. That means that, in order to have the new experience you're seeking, you need to focus first on your present-moment experience.

As we delve deeper into this journey, we'll gradually focus more and more on positive intentions and aspirations. However, the Tapping process itself starts in the now. To get the best and fastest results, use Tapping to process and release how stuck you feel, how frustrated you are about the lasting changes you want to make but have been unable to. In other words, with Tapping, we begin first with the down and dirty of daily life! By addressing and then releasing the stresses of our everyday experience, we give ourselves the time, energy, and space to create lasting change and find our flow.

That's why we start by focusing on what's most pressing right now, on what's bothering you most, big or small.

So take a moment to think—what's bothering you most right now? Not getting enough sleep? Physical pain? Work, relationship, or money stress?

Be honest here, because that's your most powerful starting point.

What's that annoying thing you just can't let go of?

What's draining your mental space and energy right now?

It's called your Most Pressing Issue (MPI), and next you'll learn to use Tapping to make that MPI shift in dramatic ways.

What Feels Real Right Now

When I talk about the MPI, people often worry that by focusing first on the negative, they're rooting themselves in it, somehow bringing it deeper into their lives.

The opposite is true. By clearing out the stress, fear, and other challenging emotions that we all naturally experience, you can more quickly clear that mental and emotional "dirt" and create more space for authentic positivity to grow and thrive.

HOW TAPPING HELPS US MOVE FORWARD AUTHENTICALLY

Tapping is an especially fast and powerful way to get quiet because it calms the nervous system and allows the body to relax. That doesn't mean that it will make everything okay. If something in your body or life doesn't "feel right," Tapping won't eliminate your discontent. Instead, Tapping eases you into the stillness you need to recognize that discomfort or discontent.

This is an important distinction because we aren't meant to find peace with everything. If there is something going on in your life that doesn't feel right, your intuition will let you know through a gut feeling or a continual thought. These messages don't come with a sense of urgency. Most often, it's a calm knowing that something isn't right and an inner calling to make a change.

Listening to your intuition takes practice, and you may stumble at first. This is why it's important to create a frequent practice around getting quiet. Over time it becomes easier, and you learn to connect with your intuition and your body more quickly and easily.

Let's Tap!

Now that you've got your MPI, it's time to get started. Here's the basic outline of how to tap.

HOW-TO-TAP VIDEO

If you learn best by watching video, you can watch this brief how-to-tap video online:

https://www.thetappingsolution.com/tapping-101

Step 1: Focus on your MPI

As you focus your attention on what's bothering you most, your MPI, ask yourself questions like *When I think about this issue, what do I feel?* Notice the feeling that you're experiencing. Are you annoyed, angry, sad, disappointed, overwhelmed, or feeling some other emotion?

You can focus on the emotion and/or what you're experiencing in your body. Ask yourself, What do I feel in my body? Do I feel tension, pain, tingling, buzzing, heat, or cold? Emptiness, numbness, or nothingness?

Pay attention to the different kinds of feedback your mind and body are giving you. There are no wrong answers here. Just try to be as specific as possible about your experience.

Step 2: Measure the intensity

Next give your MPI a number of intensity on a 0-to-10 scale. This is called the SUDS, or Subjective Units of Distress Scale.

When you focus on your MPI, how intense does the issue feel at this moment? A 10 would be the most intense you can imagine; a 0 would mean you don't feel any intensity at all.

Don't worry about getting the SUDS level exact or "right." Just follow your gut instinct.

Step 3: Craft your setup statement

With your SUDS level in mind, your next step is to craft what's called the "setup statement." This statement focuses your mind on your MPI.

The traditional EFT setup statement looks like this:

Even though I <describe your MPI>, I deeply and completely love and accept myself.

So for example, you might say, "Even though my whole body tenses every time I think about my boss, I deeply and completely accept myself."

Or, "Even though I feel so anxious about all these bills I have to pay, I love and accept myself."

Your setup statement should resonate with what you're experiencing when you begin Tapping. It's important to introduce acceptance and let your body and mind know that it's safe to relax. However, there are no "magic words" that unlock the door to getting the relief you're seeking. Your goal is to say words that have meaning to you, so if the basic setup statement doesn't ring true or feel powerful, change it.

Here are a few (of many!) variations on the basic setup statement that you can use and change to fit your experience:

Even though I <describe your MPI>, I accept myself and how I feel.

Even though I <describe your MPI>, I honor how I feel.

Even though I <describe your MPI>, it is safe for me to relax.

Even though I <describe your MPI>, it is safe for me to feel calm and confident.

Even though I <describe your MPI>, I give myself permission to relax.

Even though I <describe your MPI>, I accept how I feel and I am open to seeing this in a new way.

DO I HAVE TO SAY "I LOVE AND ACCEPT MYSELF"?

For many it feels incredibly uncomfortable and even a bit "out there" to say "I love and accept myself," especially when this is the opposite of how they may be feeling.

We have been taught that in order to achieve something, we need to fight for it. Accepting ourselves supposedly means we surrender to our flaws and never change. But it's our inability to accept ourselves that keeps us stuck. We are so busy fighting our feelings that we don't realize that the very act of fighting or trying to ignore negative feelings gives them power over us.

When we don't accept how we feel, we pile on even more emotions. Have you ever been upset at yourself for being upset? Mad at yourself for being mad? When we don't accept how we feel, we get stuck in our emotions. Over time the pile of emotions we're stuck with gets bigger and bigger.

Loving and accepting ourselves releases us from this pattern and gives us the freedom to choose a more empowering thought. Again and again I have seen the profound impact of acceptance. It is the first step to true transformation.

If you still feel uncomfortable saying the words "I love and accept myself," another statement I often use is "Even though I feel so [fill in the blank], I accept how I feel and I'm okay." You can also use EFT expert Dr. Patricia Carrington's Choices Method of countering the emotion you're feeling and adding "and I choose . . ." at the end. For example, if you're feeling overwhelmed, you could use this setup statement: "Even though I'm feeling overwhelmed, I choose to feel calm and confident."

Self-acceptance is an invitation to stop trying to change yourself into the person you wish to be, long enough to find out who you really are.

— Robert Holden

Step 4: Choose a reminder phrase(s)

The reminder phrase is short—a brief summary of the issue.

So for example, if your setup statement is about anxiety in your chest, your reminder phrases might be "This anxiety in my chest."

You repeat your reminder phrase several times when you're tapping, so you can vary it, if you like, as long as you stay focused on your MPI. In this example, you might say, "All this tension in my chest . . . So much anxiety . . . All this anxiety in my chest."

You can also pretend you are speaking to a friend and telling them why you're feeling anxious while you tap. The more specific you are the better. The point of the reminder phrase is to help you stay focusing on the thought or thoughts that are creating physical anxiety so you can begin to release the charge.

Step 5: Tap through the points

Once you have created your setup statement and reminder phrase, you're ready to start tapping.

You'll start by saying your setup statement three times, all the while tapping with two or three fingers on the Karate Chop point on your other hand. The Karate Chop point is on the side of your palm, just above the pinkie finger. You can tap with whichever hand feels most comfortable to you. Tap at a pace and force that feel right; you can't get it wrong!

After you've said the setup statement three times, you'll move on to tapping through the eight points in the Tapping sequence while saying the reminder phrase. These are the points:

- Eyebrow
- Side of eye
- Under eye
- Under nose
- Under mouth
- Collarbone
- Under arm
- Top of head

You can tap on whichever side of the body feels best to you because the same meridian channels run down both sides of the body.

Tap a handful of times at each point in the sequence. This doesn't have to be exact. If it feels right to tap 5 times, or 20 times, or 100 times on one point, then do it! The idea is to spend enough time at that point to speak your reminder phrase and let it sink in.

Again, there's no need to worry about being perfect—just do what feels right and have the experience.

Here's a diagram of the Tapping points for your reference:

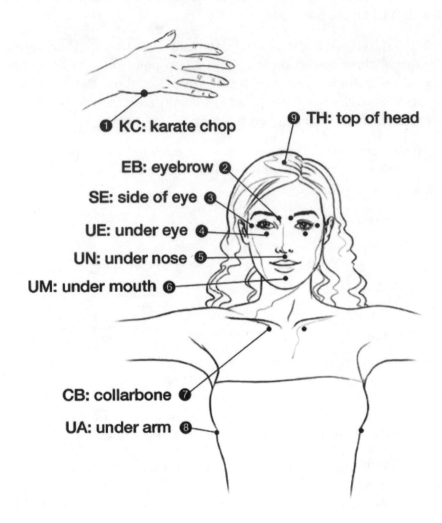

❶ KC: karate chop

❾ TH: top of head

EB: eyebrow ❷

SE: side of eye ❸

UE: under eye ❹

UN: under nose ❺

UM: under mouth ❻

CB: collarbone ❼

UA: under arm ❽

Step 6: Check in

You've now completed a round of Tapping! After repeating a few rounds of tapping through the points, it can be helpful to pause and check in with yourself.

Take a few deep breaths, and notice what's happening in your body. Did you experience a shift of any kind—in your emotions, in your thoughts, or in your body? How intense does your MPI feel on the 0-to-10 scale now?

Even smaller shifts are important to notice. They mean that Tapping is having an impact. Sometimes after doing a bit of Tapping, the intensity may increase or shift to the body, creating physical sensations, such as pain or yawning, burping, and more. If that happens, keep tapping! You're getting to the core issue, and relief will follow. If there's no change, that's fine, too. Often people need more than one round of Tapping to experience relief, especially when they are new to the process or haven't tapped in a while.

YAWNING, SIGHING, BURPING, AND MORE

People often ask if they're doing something wrong, since each time they tap, they begin yawning or experiencing other physical effects. These are all good signs! They're ways that your body is relaxing, moving and releasing energy, and letting go. When you tap, make a point of noticing all the ways your body responds.

Step 7: Test your progress

Once the intensity of your MPI has decreased, it's time to test your results. You can do this by refocusing your attention on your MPI.

If focusing on your MPI still feels emotionally charged, continue tapping through a few more rounds using the same language, and see if you can clear your MPI altogether.

Or you might find that as you think about your MPI, your emotions change. Instead of feeling anxious, for instance, you now feel angry. That's great! That's an indication that you're getting to the root of your MPI. In that case, you can move on and tap on your anger. If, while tapping on that anger, you find that it's masking yet another emotion, like sadness, go ahead and tap on that sadness, as well.

Just keep tapping through the layers of your emotions until you experience the relief you're seeking.

Aren't Emotions a Good Thing? Why Do We Tap on Releasing Them?

People sometimes ask why we focus on releasing emotions when we're tapping.

Aren't emotions a good thing?

Yes, they absolutely are!

Our goal with Tapping is never to stop feeling our emotions. Instead, Tapping helps us acknowledge how we're feeling, and then feel that *more* fully. When we can do that, our emotions naturally progress. For instance, if you tap on anger, that anger may then turn into sadness, which then becomes compassion.

As a result of this emotional processing and release, which often happens faster with Tapping, we become more present in the moment. That presence then supports you in creating lasting change and finding your flow.

Switching from the "Negative" to the "Positive"

Throughout the book, each Tapping script begins with the "negative," which is really just your present moment truth, a statement that includes your MPI, and any related challenging emotions and beliefs. Most of the time, I'll end with at least one "positive" round of tapping, which presents a new way of moving forward.

For example, if you were tapping on anxiety you're feeling around a presentation, you might end your Tapping with phrases like, "I can release this anxiety now," "I can focus on practicing," "I'm safe being seen and heard by all those people," and so on.

As a general rule, it's best to get the intensity of the negative down to a 5 out of 10 before moving on to the positive, and then to keep tapping on the positive until the negative emotional charge has decreased to a 3 or lower.

MY TOP 10 TAPPING TIPS

- *Start with where you are.* There is power in asking yourself questions to get clear on what's happening beneath the surface, but this kind of clarity doesn't often appear when we are feeling overwhelmed or frustrated. Always start by tapping on how you're feeling. Instead of trying to analyze the emotion(s) or physical sensation you're experiencing, or assign a reason why you're feeling a certain way, simply focus on the emotion and/or feeling itself. For example, begin tapping on the anxiety or anger or frustration you're feeling, instead of immediately trying to explain why you're feeling it. As you continue tapping through the points, clarity (and relief!) will follow.

- *Be specific.* The Tapping Meditation at the end of each chapter and the extended scripts in the Appendix are powerful guides. For the best results, be specific to your own unique feelings and thoughts while you tap. You can use my scripts to help you gain momentum and then begin inserting your own words.

- *It's not about the words you say; it's about how you feel.* Tapping and repeating phrases out loud or in your mind helps you stay focused on the experience you want to relieve, but those words aren't always necessary. If you find yourself in emotional distress but unsure of what to say, just begin to tap!

- *Only move from "negative" to "positive," empowering statements when it feels authentic to how you're feeling.* It's often tempting to ignore how we feel—afraid, worried, disappointed, and so on—and try to jump into positive affirmations. When we do this without addressing our resistance—which shows up as the "negative" emotions we're actually feeling—the positive intentions have no impact because they're not authentic to how we're feeling. If you say something positive and it doesn't feel right, do more tapping on the negative. When the negative loses its power, you'll have room for a positive, empowering belief to take root.

- *Follow what feels the best.* People often share how they have been using Tapping, and then they ask, "Am I doing it right?" I usually respond, "Does it make you feel better?" If the answer is yes, then you've got this! I'll share what has worked for my clients and for me, but ultimately this is about what feels best to you.

- *Celebrate every shift.* Did you go from a 10 to a 9 in intensity? Celebrate! When you celebrate a shift, it reaffirms to your mind that it's safe to begin to let go of these thoughts and emotions that don't serve you. It also makes it easier to continue tapping when you feel encouraged by the shift, no matter how small it feels.

- *Ask questions.* As you tap through how you're feeling, clarity often arrives easily. With deeply rooted emotions and beliefs, the process can take longer. When that happens, it can be helpful to ask questions. My two favorite questions are, "What is the downside of letting this go?" and "What does this feeling remind me of?" Asking different questions while you tap helps you to make discoveries and gain clarity. Throughout this book I share questions to reflect on. When we replace criticism with curiosity we begin to gain the clarity we hoped for.

- *Explore metaphors.* Another way to dig deeper into more challenging issues is with metaphors. If you are experiencing a pain in your neck, ask yourself, "*Who* is a pain in my neck?" If you're holding on to weight in your stomach, ask yourself, "Is there an idea I need to give birth to?" Often the body acts like a metaphor for what we are experiencing emotionally. I once volunteered at an elder home where a woman in her 80s had a pain in her back. When I asked her if anyone stabbed her in the back, she didn't hesitate to respond. As we tapped on that experience, the pain in her back disappeared. This is not always the case, but it's always worth exploring and can provide interesting insights.

- *Let yourself release and transform gently and gradually.* I use the word *maybe* a lot in my Tapping Meditations. I find it's especially powerful when the emotional intensity (SUDS) has gone down to somewhere around 4 to 6 out of 10. When we're not yet ready to embrace a new way of thinking or to let an emotion go fully, the word *maybe* can act as a soft transition, providing the time and space to release and transform at our own pace and on our own terms.

- *After Tapping, pay attention to any thoughts and ideas that surface.* When we calm our body and mind, we can more easily connect to intuition. If a decision doesn't feel right, Tapping won't erase that feeling, it simply helps you to feel calm and centered enough to hear your intuition say, "No, this doesn't feel right," or "Yes, go for it!" Give yourself a moment after Tapping to check in with yourself and hear the whispers of your intuition.

Now that you've got a sense of how to tap, it's time to dive into our journey. Let's get started!

You can't hate
yourself HAPPY,
you can't criticize
yourself THin,
you can't SHAME
yourself wealthy.
All CHANGe begins
with SELF-love
and SELF-CAre.

Chapter 1

Why We Stay Stuck

Around 5,040 days had to pass before I noticed the pattern that was keeping me stuck. That pattern, which I now call the *pattern of panic*, began when I was 14 years old and just starting my first diet. Before long, I was cycling through fad diets, then fad exercise routines, desperate to transform my body.

Each time, I'd follow a strict plan and lose some weight. Eventually, though, I'd get exhausted and resort to my old habit of binge eating. Standing in front of the cupboard, consuming entire boxes of "healthy" bars and nuts, I felt relieved, even empowered. I was rebelling, taking my power back from a society that seemed ashamed of me for not being a size 2.

Soon, though, my elation would turn into regret and disappointment. Feeling defeated, I'd then find a new, even better fad diet, an even *more* effective fat-burning exercise routine to follow.

Each time I cycled through this pattern, I told myself that if I really, really, *really* wanted to lose weight, then my desperation would be strong enough to make me change. I told myself that I couldn't let up, that I *had to* be hard on myself. That's what made me a smart, self-aware person. All I needed, really, was the right plan.

I soon became a self-help junkie. I read books and attended seminars, feverishly looking for someone to just tell me how to end my struggle. The more I focused on "fixing" myself, the more flaws I found. The more I read, the more pressure I felt to do things perfectly.

My initial struggle was with my body and self-image. Maybe you can relate, or perhaps you feel stuck when it comes to your finances, your relationship status, or your career path. When we are faced with a struggle, something we desperately want to change but isn't, we tend to do one thing: stress!

Overwhelmed by my own stress and panic, I grew increasingly disconnected from my own body and my own intuition. Surely, I kept telling myself, someone out there had the perfect plan for me. If I just kept looking, and kept being hard on myself, I'd finally succeed at transforming my body, and then my life.

It's what we often do when we're stuck in the pattern of panic. We hold on to that panic, thinking that if we could criticize ourselves enough then maybe something will change. We try to hate ourselves happy. We try to stress our way to resolution without realizing that very stress is what's keeping us stuck. We then look for solutions outside of ourselves. We search for a "fix," when what we truly need is to go within.

This pattern is a self-perpetuating cycle that continues until we take a deeper look at why our past attempts to get unstuck either haven't worked or haven't proven sustainable.

Why We Stay Stuck

Let's face it, we *know* when we're stuck. Even when we hesitate to admit it, we can usually *tell* when we're in a rut. We also know that making some sort of change is the only way out.

At some point we dive headfirst into making the changes we're sure we need to make. The problem is, the changes we're making come from a place of panic. We pile extra pressure on ourselves and become even more self-critical. As that panic continues to fuel our critical voice, we say things to ourselves like, "Get your act together, you should be further along by now, what's wrong with you?" Then we write that list of goals, start the diet, or commit to following this or that exercise/budgeting/career/you-name-it plan.

At first it may feel invigorating. Already we can see our lives turning around. It's going to be great! Then time goes by, and we begin to realize that creating lasting change is harder than we expected. It takes time, patience, perseverance. We get tired. We feel resentful, defeated by our lack of tangible progress. Before long, we begin to wonder, "Is it really worth it?" Truthfully, we still feel stressed, uncertain, and yes, panicked that we actually are as stuck as we feared.

Eventually, fatigue and exasperation win, and we revert back to old self-sabotaging patterns. We then find ourselves back in the same cycle—feeling stuck, then panicked, desperate for change that we can't seem to create or sustain.

Once we've navigated this frustrating cycle repeatedly, we begin to wonder if we'll ever get unstuck. We feel worn down, frustrated, angry. We've gotten used to living in a state of controlled panic, yet we can feel its effects. That underlying panic causes stress, continuously taxing our health, wellness, relationships, even our work and finances.

In spite of it all, we somehow manage to hold on to a tiny voice inside us. It's that quiet whisper telling us to keep trying, to keep believing that we will get unstuck, and rediscover our flow . . . somehow . . . someday.

The question is, how can we get unstuck and rediscover our flow—a state of ease as we navigate change—not just briefly but for the long term?

The answer is the same one we've had all along. We get unstuck by embracing change, but not in the ways we've attempted in the past. To manifest lasting and fulfilling change, we first have to re-create our entire experience around change.

We'll begin that process by first understanding the role that the brain plays in keeping us stuck.

The Brain's Safety Bias

The primitive human brain was not wired to value change, growth, and flow. Instead, the primitive brain, also called the unconscious brain, is engineered to support survival above all else. As a result, avoiding pain is a far bigger focus than seeking reward or creating pleasure.

That may sound limiting, but the brain's singular focus on safety has served us well. After all, it was only a few hundred years ago when day-to-day life revolved almost exclusively around surviving. If you didn't stay alert in the woods or mountains or vast, open plains, you could easily end up face-to-face with a startled bear, hungry lion, or venomous snake.

Given that this was true for the majority of human existence to date, the brain developed to be more focused on negativity—what could go wrong, be dangerous, and so on—than on positivity, such as what may be beneficial, enjoyable, and so on. Historically speaking, it was the cautious person who walked in fear who was most likely to survive. The unfortunate ones who wandered aimlessly in the wild were far more likely to get eaten.

That's why the brain evolved to overestimate threats and underestimate benefits. Studies have even shown that the brain recognizes fear in other people's faces faster than happiness.[1] It's how we're wired.

The Brain and Body on Fear

The brain's bias toward negativity quickly impacts the physical body. When we feel emotions like fear, the amygdala, a part of the brain responsible for survival instincts, essentially sounds an internal alarm. When this happens, the brain instructs the body to start releasing chemicals, including the "stress hormone" cortisol.

As cortisol floods the body, our senses are heightened, making us more alert and better able to run faster, climb higher, and perform other potentially life-saving functions. Since the brain is channeling our energy toward survival, fewer of our internal resources are available for nonessential functions, such as creativity, complex problem solving, nurturing, digestion, and more.

This entire process, which starts in the brain and quickly spreads throughout the body, is commonly known as the *stress response*, or the *fight-or-flight* response.

The Primitive Brain in a Modern World

Throughout most of human history, the primitive brain and the *stress response* it initiates have proven critical to our individual and collective survival. Today, however, as we navigate daily life protected by thick walls, modern conveniences, and abundant technology, our needs are different. We can spend far more time and energy on thriving and far less on basic survival. Nonetheless, we're still being guided by the same primitive brain we had hundreds of years ago.

The truth is, navigating modern life with a primitive brain can be limiting. While it was fantastic that our brains learned to detect that lion creeping in the tall grass after we narrowly escaped the first time, the brain's "negativity bias" often seems excessive today.[2] As one example, you might not need your primitive brain to prevent you from speaking up in a meeting because you were teased for speaking up in elementary school—but it will. Similarly, you might not want that one poor math grade in middle school to keep you from effectively managing your finances—but again, it will.

The primitive brain's survival bias is so well honed that every time we have an experience that creates a strong negative emotional response, it creates new neural pathways. Those pathways are a kind of hardwiring that protect us from experiencing those same challenges—like speaking up or doing math—again. It's the exact same process that the primitive brain underwent to protect us from that lion creeping through the tall grass.

The question is, are those experiences equal? Is being teased for speaking up in elementary school as dangerous as being surprised by a hungry lion? Of course not! Unfortunately, the primitive brain can't tell the difference.

Why Change Feels So Hard

So how does this safety bias affect us when we're trying to get unstuck?

The primitive brain's bias comes into play when we try to create the change that's necessary to get unstuck. That's because, according to the primitive brain, change is unsafe.

This blanket bias against change may seem counterintuitive when we're talking about positive change that can help us get unstuck. However, this is the *primitive* brain we're talking about. Its programming is basic and primal, so it doesn't differentiate between positive and negative change. By definition, change means uncertainty, and by default, uncertainty is unsafe. As far as the primitive brain is concerned, the fact that a known experience, such as being stuck, has not interfered with survival is sufficient evidence to categorize it as safe.

In other words, across the board, the brain prefers the certainty of your current experience (which it sees as safe, simply because you're still alive) over the uncertainty of change (which it sees as unsafe, simply because it's unknown). That's why change feels so hard—because the brain and body are working against us when we most need their support.

When we attempt to grow, expand, and evolve, the primitive brain rushes in to protect us from potential new threats. It fires off warning signals, telling the brain and body that we are unsafe. That's how the *pattern of panic* works.

Unfortunately, getting out of the pattern of panic can be challenging. Since our panic registers on emotional, mental, and physical levels, we can't simply talk ourselves out of it.

Tapping into the Primitive Brain

The good news is, we have 24/7 access to a powerful resource for rewiring the primitive brain—the body!

Multiple studies have used high-resolution fMRI scans to observe specific points on the body, called acupoints. These points act like gateways to the primitive brain. By tapping on these points while processing and releasing our negative emotions and limiting beliefs, as we do when we're tapping, we can send the primitive brain positive, calming messages.

One of the most exciting aspects of tapping is that it's a simple practice that anyone can use. Once you know tapping, you always have a tool to support you through times of stress. It's incredibly self-empowering!

WANT MORE RESEARCH?

If you're interested in reading more about dozens of other studies that have demonstrated how effective tapping is for a wide range of disorders and conditions, you can visit www.thetappingsolution.com/science-research or check out my brother Nick Ortner's *New York Times* best-selling book *The Tapping Solution: A Revolutionary System for Stress-Free Living.*

Where Lasting Change Begins

I had been tapping for over a year when I finally began using it to address the pattern of panic that had kept me stuck since my first diet at age 14.

The turning point began one day when I was attending a conference after my brother and I had released *The Tapping Solution* documentary film. By that point I'd done online interviews and Tapping Meditations, and we'd begun to attract an online audience.

Before the event began, the volunteer who was registering me shared how much she'd gotten from my Tapping videos, and then said something I'll never forget:

"You're bigger than I thought you'd be."

I smiled, hoping she wasn't noticing the shame rising up through my throat, burning my cheeks a molten red. In that single moment, she confirmed every fear I'd ever had. As far as my primitive brain was concerned, she'd just told me that I wasn't good enough to be seen—and wouldn't be, until I lost weight.

In a state of shock, I walked over to my brother Nick and told him what had happened. After commenting on how rude that was, he very gently said, "You've been struggling with this for a long time, and it obviously causes you a lot of emotional pain. Why don't you try Tapping?" To be honest, even though I had seen over and over again the power of Tapping, my first reaction was to roll my eyes. I was still so brainwashed to believe weight loss was only about our ability to push hard and stick with a diet. We live in a society that tells us that lasting change only happens when we push hard enough for it.

Later that evening, though, I let his words sink in and realized he had a good point. I was tired—tired of trying so hard and nothing working. I was tired of how much my insecurities consumed my thoughts, and of being disappointed after each new plan failed to produce the lasting change I desired.

I had an honest conversation with myself and realized the panic, worry, and brute force I was trying to use to change just wasn't working.

In the days and weeks that followed, as I used Tapping to address my relationship with food and my body, I discovered something that surprised me. My problem wasn't binge eating or the size or shape of my body. It was how I'd been treating myself. It was the decade-plus I'd spent trying to hate myself happy.

Instead of focusing my Tapping exclusively on binge eating and getting motivated to exercise, my attention began to turn toward self-love and self-acceptance. Before long, I began to feel more at ease in my body than I had in many years. A month later, I'd lost 10 pounds without dieting or depriving myself. I felt calmer, more confident and empowered around food than I ever had. I was also exercising, but in pleasurable, enjoyable ways.

I was making changes that brought me peace, joy, and ease. Thanks to Tapping, I'd discovered my flow around my body, food, and exercise. My entire life did begin to feel different, but not because I was a size 2 (I wasn't). My circumstances, my career, finances, and love life were still far from perfect, but I felt more at peace than I had in a very long time.

As weeks turned into months, I realized that my primitive brain's safety bias had prevented me from feeling good in my own skin. For years I'd told myself that losing weight was the key to being seen in my career, relationships, and beyond. For years I'd told myself that once I'd lost weight, I could speak my mind and be myself. While the conscious brain might have found that exciting and liberating, to my primitive brain, that additional exposure was threatening. To keep me safe, my primitive brain wanted and needed me to continue binge eating so I didn't venture into new and unknown territory where I might get hurt.

With Tapping, I was able to release my limiting beliefs and deep-seated fears. I was able to reassure my primitive brain that I was safe being seen. As I began to transform my inner life, releasing anxiety, fear, and other emotions in the process, I easily found my flow. Because I'd used Tapping to shed my panic, I could get in touch with myself on a deeper level, and move forward in positive, empowering ways.

Although my primitive brain is still hard at work, often pointing out new reasons for me to feel afraid, now that I understand what it's up to, I can regain my calm without resorting to self-sabotaging behavior.

The Power of Joy

When you imagine embracing the unknown and celebrating change, do you feel excited, even energized?

How, then, do you feel when that uncertainty and change enter your life in real, tangible terms—in the form of a sudden job change or a shift in relationship, finances, family, health, or similar? Do you dive into real-life challenges with change, or do you hesitate, whether by delaying decision making, procrastinating, worrying excessively, or something else?

Let's face it, change and uncertainty are fun in theory, but often scary when they enter our daily lives. Now that you know that the anxiety you feel around change and the unknown is just the primitive brain tainting your relationship with change, stop for a second and try to imagine what tangible, real-life change might feel like . . . *without* the panic.

Could creating change in order to get unstuck be a source of joy? Could it boost your creativity . . . abundance . . . even love? Could making changes be uplifting and inspiring . . . even when things don't go exactly as planned?

The first step in re-creating your experience around change is noticing how and where you experience panic in your body. When you focus on feeling stuck, do you feel tightness in your chest, a knot in your stomach, pain in your back, neck, or elsewhere? Do you feel sensations like hot or cold, buzzing or throbbing? If so, where in your body do you feel them?

As you begin to notice how panic manifests in your body, keep in mind that panic doesn't always feel frantic or frenetic. Most of us have gotten used to absorbing our panic, so it can show up in the body as dull, persistent, numb, or even heavy or slow feelings.

As you move forward, continue to notice when and how panic shows up in your body. That new awareness will be enormously helpful as we continue to break out of the pattern of panic. First, though, we'll look at where we're going by considering what flow is and what flow isn't.

Time for the End-of-Chapter Tapping Meditation!

It's time to use Tapping to begin quieting the pattern of panic. Before moving on to the next chapter, use the Chapter 1 Tapping Meditation that follows.

If you're new to Tapping, first refer to the Tapping Quick Start Guide starting on page xix.

CHAPTER 1 TAPPING MEDITATION: QUIETING THE PANIC

Close your eyes for a moment and focus your attention on feeling stuck. As you do that, mentally scan your body. Notice any sensations you feel. These are likely ways that your body is absorbing panic.

Does the word panic *not resonate with you? Maybe it shows up as frustration or anger. Use the word that most resonates.*

Focus on where in your body you feel the panic most intensely. Rate the intensity of that panic on a scale of 0 to 10, with 10 being the highest intensity you can imagine.

With that panic in mind, let's start tapping.

As you tap through the rounds, feel free to substitute words that reflect your experience. Also be aware of how your experience shifts during and after tapping.

Take a deep breath.

Begin tapping on the Karate Chop point.

Karate Chop *(repeat three times)*: Even though I have all this panic in my body when I think about needing to make a change, I accept myself and how I feel.

Eyebrow: This panic

Side of Eye: It's in my body

Under Eye: I can feel it

Under Nose: I feel it in <area of body where you feel it most>

Under Mouth: It feels like <describe it—buzzing, tightness, etc.>

Collarbone: This panic

Under Arm: It's in my body

Top of Head: I feel it

Eyebrow: This panic

Side of Eye: It's overwhelming

Under Eye: It's been with me for so long

Under Nose: Something has to change

Under Mouth: I've been trying for so long

Collarbone: And nothing seems to work

Under Arm: So I feel all this worry

Top of Head: All this frustration

Eyebrow: This panic in my body

Side of Eye: Part of me wants to let it go

Under Eye: Another part of me wants to hold on to it

Under Nose: Because I have to worry

Under Mouth: And panic

Collarbone: To make a change

Under Arm: That's what I've been taught

Top of Head: Is that really true?

Eyebrow: I honor how hard this has been

Side of Eye: It's safe to feel this panic

Under Eye: Even though I just want it to go away

Under Nose: I can let myself feel this panic

Under Mouth: It's safe to feel this panic

Collarbone: I don't have to fight it

Under Arm: I honor how I feel

Top of Head: It's safe to feel this

Eyebrow: I can begin to let go of this panic

Side of Eye: I can let myself relax now

Under Eye: And let go of this panic

Under Nose: I'm safe without this panic

Under Mouth: I don't need this panic to stay safe

Collarbone: I can let it go now

Under Arm: I can feel calm in my body

Top of Head: I can trust that I'm safe

Eyebrow: I'm safe without this panic

Side of Eye: I can feel quiet and relaxed now

Under Eye: I can let my body rest

Under Nose: And let my body feel better

Under Mouth: Releasing this panic now

Collarbone: Relaxing in this moment

Under Arm: I'm safe

Top of Head: I can relax now

Eyebrow: I can feel good in this moment

Side of Eye: Things don't have to be perfect

Under Eye: For me to relax and feel calmer

Under Nose: I can feel at peace in my mind

Under Mouth: And at peace in my heart

Collarbone: And at peace in my body

Under Arm: I'm safe

Top of Head: I can relax now

Eyebrow: I can trust this good feeling

Side of Eye: And let myself feel peaceful now

Under Eye: I can let my body rest

Under Nose: And let myself feel better

Under Mouth: Relaxing in this moment

Collarbone: Feeling calm now

Under Arm: Letting my body and mind relax

Top of Head: Feeling at peace now

Take a deep breath and check in with yourself. How has the panic you felt in your body shifted? Rate its intensity on a scale of 0 to 10.

Note: If your panicked feeling has shifted, either in sensation (from tightness to tingling, for example) or to a new spot in your body, continue tapping until you feel peaceful.

Keep tapping for as long as you like.

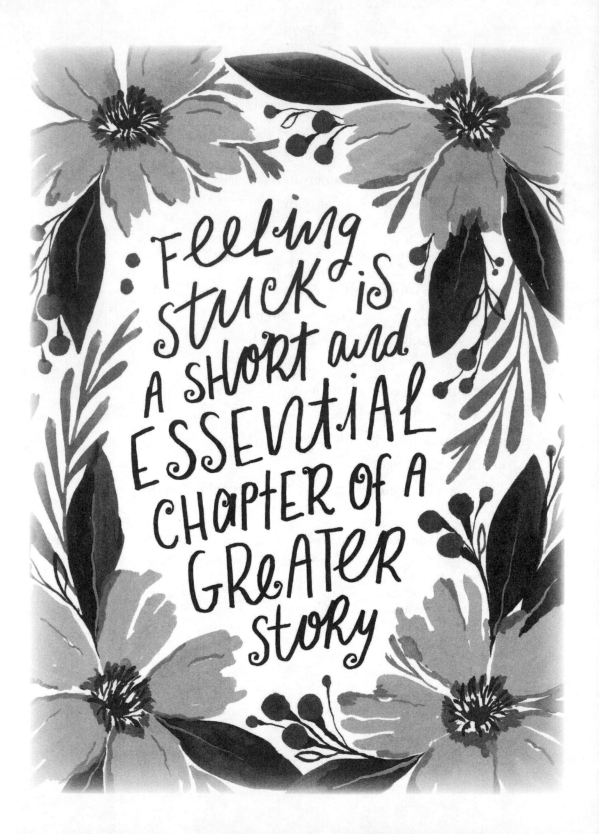

Feeling stuck is a short and essential chapter of a greater story

Chapter 2

Moving toward Flow

Webster defines flow as "gliding along smoothly."

Nature demonstrates this perfectly. Spring glides smoothly into summer, summer into autumn, and autumn into winter. Each season flows into the next without struggle or resistance.

To create more flow in your life is to create more ease. The same way nature isn't always in a state of spring (a time for new growth and blooming), flow isn't always about creating and achieving. It's also about recognizing when it's time to let go, the way we see the autumn trees do so beautifully every fall. Flow is about ending the struggle to always go, do, and be more so that we can sense when to take action and when to rest and reset.

Whether flow shows up as letting go of a past love or pursing a big goal, being in flow means you experience more ease through the different seasons of life. When we quiet self-criticism and address our fears with Tapping, as we'll continue to do throughout this journey, we can commune with our soul and learn how to better navigate our own path. We can find our flow.

Flow That Ebbs and Flows

One of the perks of doing the work I do is having had the chance to meet some of my greatest spiritual mentors, from Louise Hay to Wayne Dyer. Over the years many of them have been candid about those times when they felt stuck, and how they then returned to a state of flow.

One of those moments happened while filming the documentary *The Tapping Solution*. During that time, we flew to Austin, Texas, to interview Dr. Joe Vitale, who was featured in the movie *The Secret*. As I sat behind the camera asking him why he personally uses Tapping and recommends it to others, he said something that has stayed with me:

"We are always going to have problems. That's part of the human experience. The question is, what are we going to do about them?"

His answer highlights what I've experienced in myself and seen repeatedly in others: Tapping brings us back to ourselves when we are faced with a challenge so we can handle it with more ease. It allows us to resume flow when we otherwise might get stuck.

I have yet to meet every single person on this planet, so I cannot say with certainty that *no one* stays in a constant state of flow. Maybe the Dalai Lama or the Pope or some guru who meditates incessantly has figured it out. I myself have never experienced nor met anyone who never gets stuck.

So the question this book answers is not, "How can I always stay in a perfect state of flow?" The question we're addressing instead is:

How can I bring myself back into flow when I'm feeling stuck?

We begin to uncover the answer by looking at how we relate to our emotions.

Flowing through Emotions

Too often we judge ourselves for being stuck and for feeling negative emotions like anxiety, fear, and worry. Those judgments are one of the biggest reasons we stay stuck.

Instead of accepting that being stuck is part of our human experience, we make it wrong. We think we should know better. We tell ourselves we shouldn't ever feel stuck because we've read so many books, attended workshops, and dabbled in meditation.

These judgments keep us stuck because of how they impact our self-esteem. I noticed that in myself when I was first introduced to Tapping. At first I couldn't say the traditional setup statement, which is: *Even though [state the problem], I love and accept myself.*

Each time, the words *I love and accept myself* would get caught in my throat, and tears would roll down my face. I had worked so hard at trying to change and improve myself that self-acceptance felt counterintuitive. Why would I love and accept myself when I so desperately wanted to change?

My quest for self-help turned into self-punishment because I was missing a key ingredient: self-compassion. I was great at feeling compassion for others, but refused to give any to myself. That refusal kept me stuck in the pattern of panic.

> *If your compassion does not include yourself, it is incomplete.*
> — Jack Kornfield

One of the ways to notice your own judgments about your experience and emotions is by becoming more aware of how and when the words *should* and *shouldn't* show up. For example, you might hear yourself say things like:

"I shouldn't feel this way."

"I should have healed this by now."

"I should be further along by now."

"I should be doing more."

What do you say to yourself when you feel "bad" emotions or admit to yourself that you're stuck? Write anything that comes to mind:

_____

_____

_____

The Three Ways We Relate to Our Emotions

We tend to address emotions in three main ways. Only one of those ways supports us in getting unstuck and finding our flow.

As we've seen, one thing we often do with our feelings is deny and judge them with all those "should" statements. We chastise ourselves for being too sensitive. We may then rely on activities that numb us out, like emotional eating or binge-watching television shows, to avoid those emotions. Distraction feels like a relief because we are scared to face how we feel.

When we aren't willing to face how we feel, the body may try to get our attention through anxiety we feel in our chest, insomnia, physical pain, and more. It's the body saying, *Hey! You're holding on to something that's hurting you. Pay attention!*

Another way we address our emotions is by feeding them. We run through what happened in our mind over and over again and get angrier and angrier. We don't want to let go of the anger because we fear what may happen if we do. We tell ourselves that we need that anger—or sadness, or fear, or anxiety—in order to change or simply to keep ourselves safe.

The tricky part, as we've seen, is that for a short time this strategy may work. You may take action as a result of your anger, fear, or other feelings. However, when your action is motivated by panic or other negative emotions, you will feel like you're walking through molasses to get to where you want to go. Your progress will be slow and frustrating.

Other times, this habit of reliving and feeding our emotions keeps us feeling frozen. We hold on to these feelings, hoping that by focusing on them, we can prevent being hurt again in the future. We hold on to prevent a pain that's already happened, and we stay stuck.

You're also more likely to make poor decisions because you're so deeply rooted in negative emotion that you can't think clearly.

The third and most constructive way we can relate to our emotions is by acknowledging and accepting them. When we do this, we can move through our emotions and learn from them.

This is the only way of relating to our emotions that leaves space for us to find our flow. That's because we don't get stuck in pushing emotions away or holding on to them. We move through them just as nature moves through the seasons.

To find our flow, we have to let our emotions flow.

While it is possible to move through our emotions on our own, Tapping provides direct access to the primitive brain and the body, both of which store emotion. As a result, with Tapping we're able to feel and release emotions more quickly and easily.

Even the act of telling yourself you need to process this emotion and learn from it before your 6 P.M. yoga class is a command fueled with judgment and criticism.

It all starts by acknowledging that where are you are and how you're feeling is okay. We'll continue to do that as we move through this journey.

Positive Thinking: When It Works (and When It Doesn't)

Isn't it better to focus on the positive? Isn't tapping on affirmations and mantras a better starting point?

I've heard these questions from clients so many times, I'm going to share something else about this topic.

Of course no one consciously *wants* to get stuck in negative thoughts or emotions. The fact is, though, we all have them sometimes. By trying to ignore negative feelings or judge ourselves for having them, we simply give them permission to control us and our behavior. When we resist our negative thoughts and emotions, when we try to force ourselves into positivity, our negative emotions gain more power over us, not less.

Anger is a great example. If we're angry, we can't just decide to stop feeling anger. We can't force ourselves not to be angry. We need to feel and move through our anger. We have to find a way to "blow off steam" before we can relax and calm down.

Tapping gives us an incredibly fast and effective way to move through our negative thoughts and emotions so we can then let them go. At that point, once our emotional "slate" has been cleared, we can authentically root ourselves in positive thoughts, emotions, affirmations, and mantras.

As I've mentioned, the best way to experience less negativity is to tap on the negative aspects of your life—your stress, frustration, worry, and so on. As you tap and lessen the intensity of those negative thoughts and emotions, you'll be able to do Tapping using positive statements, which will further lower your stress and enable you to find your flow.

Embracing the Magic

Now that we've defined flow and looked at some of the ways we block flow, you're probably still thinking something like, Okay, but I still need to create lasting change. I still need to find true love . . . transform my career . . . finances . . . health and body . . . and more!

We all have goals that we want to work toward. We'll address those later in the journey. Sometimes we're clear on those goals from the start, and sometimes we discover them as we move forward. Either way, it can feel frustrating to focus on spiritual principles like flow when you need and want love or money or a new job or house. We've all been there!

When we stay singularly focused on tangible external goals, though, we tend to stay stuck. We default to self-criticism, which leads us back into the pattern of panic. That's when we're our least productive, our least creative, our least resourceful. The anxiety and panic we feel around not having achieved our goals yet may then impact our physical well-being, which contributes to the frustrating cycle we're trying to escape.

When we release ourselves from panic and allow ourselves to feel what we're feeling, we give ourselves the chance to rediscover our flow. We become process oriented, rather than goal oriented. We find joy and meaning in the little steps we take each day. Ironically, it's that shift toward growth and evolution and away from outcomes that often allows us to realize our desires more easily and faster, as well.

Simply put, if it isn't pleasurable, it's not sustainable.

That's the magic of falling in love with the process of finding flow. We open ourselves to the magic the Universe has to offer us, and without even noticing, we achieve our goals faster and more easily than we ever imagined.

Your Greater Story Is Unfolding Here and Now

Pick up a biography or watch a biographical movie. Notice the moments when this or that famous person felt stuck, lost, and disappointed. It was in those moments that they had to make a choice. They could let their life's story be about how stuck and hopeless they felt, or they could accept the challenge and discover that they are stronger than their circumstances.

Being dissatisfied with life, feeling stuck, and longing for more is one of those pivotal moments for you, too. It's one chapter of the bigger, longer, greater story that is your life. One day you'll look back at this very moment and understand how even when you felt stuck and lost, there was magic all around you, moving you closer to where you most longed to be.

Trust that magic. Dance with it. Let it guide you. You're on your way, even now.

Time for the End-of-Chapter Tapping Meditation!

In the next chapter, we'll take a closer look at an important piece of the pattern of panic—the role of the critical voice.

Before you move to Chapter 3, make sure to complete the Chapter 2 Tapping Meditation.

If you're new to Tapping, first refer to the Quick Start Tapping Guide starting on page xix.

CHAPTER 2 TAPPING MEDITATION: WELCOMING MORE EASE INTO YOUR LIFE

The primitive brain is so oriented toward negativity that we sometimes hesitate to trust that we can realize fulfilling, lasting change *and* experience more flow, or ease, in our lives.

When you imagine creating the change you desire, how much mistrust do you feel around the idea that you could also experience more ease, or flow, on a regular basis? On some level do you believe that "other people" can receive abundance, in its many forms, and experience more flow? How unsafe does it feel to trust that you can create the change you desire *and* experience more flow?

Rate the intensity of your resistance—your mistrust and so on—on a scale of 0 to 10.

Take a deep breath.

Begin tapping on the Karate Chop point.

Karate Chop *(repeat three times)*: Even though I've been taught that I have to push and suffer to create lasting change, I accept myself and I'm open to a new way.

Eyebrow: If I want to create lasting change

Side of Eye: I have to suffer through it

Under Eye: Change takes willpower

Under Nose: And I never seem to have enough willpower

Under Mouth: I keep pushing myself to change

Collarbone: And nothing has been working

Under Arm: It's not safe to expect more flow and ease in my life

Top of Head: I'll be too disappointed when it doesn't happen

Eyebrow: It's not safe to trust I'll find my flow

Side of Eye: It's not safe to trust I can have ease and lasting change, too

Under Eye: That's too much

Under Nose: I've never been one of those people

Under Mouth: Who gets what they want easily

Collarbone: Anything worthwhile has to be hard

Under Arm: I can't trust that I'll find my flow and create lasting change

Top of Head: It's too much

Eyebrow: My life just isn't like that

Side of Eye: Good things are always hard

Under Eye: I can't expect more ease, too

Under Nose: I can't expect to find my flow and create this change

Under Mouth: It's too much

Collarbone: Is it really, though?

Under Arm: Maybe I can find my flow?

Top of Head: Maybe I can experience more ease, too?

Eyebrow: But I can't let go of this belief

Side of Eye: That good things have to be hard

Under Eye: Maybe I can, though

Under Nose: Maybe I can try to let more ease into my life

Under Mouth: As I move toward the lasting change I desire

Collarbone: I'm safe believing that I can experience more ease, too

Under Arm: Maybe good things can feel easy, too

Top of Head: It's safe to trust in flow

Eyebrow: I can trust that I can experience more ease

Side of Eye: And create the change I desire, too

Under Eye: It's safe to relax

Under Nose: It's safe to feel good

Under Mouth: I can feel excited about this!

Collarbone: I can relax and trust in flow

Under Arm: I can welcome more ease into my life

Top of Head: And let that ease fill me with joy

Eyebrow: All this ease

Side of Eye: All this flow

Under Eye: I embrace it

Under Nose: I welcome it into my daily experience

Under Mouth: I can trust the joy it brings

Collarbone: And allow myself to feel safe within my flow

Under Arm: I can relax now

Top of Head: I can feel this joy now

Take a deep, relaxing breath. Check back in on the intensity of your resistance around embracing flow and ease as you create lasting change. Keep tapping until you feel the desired level of joy and peace.

Step 1: Trigger

Something or someone triggers the pattern of panic...

- We compare ourselves with others and decide we're somehow lacking

- We decide that we need to change; that we should be further along by now

Step 2: Critical Voice

We try to motivate ourselves though self-criticism and "tough love," aka shame:

"Get yourself together!"
"You should be further along by now!"
"What's wrong with you?"

The Pattern of Panic

The self-sabotaging cycle that makes positive change seem unsustainable or out of reach

Step 4: Rebellion

- We rebel, and indulge is self-sabotaging behaviors to ease stress (over eating/spending, binge watching TV, binge surfing the Internet, etc.)

- We procrastinate on important tasks that support the change we desire

- We talk ourselves out of the change we desire because creating that change feels too hard.

Step 3: Action!

- We take action, but from a place of frustration and panic, relying on strict rules and plans and expecting nothing less than perfection

- We make some progress. It's working!

- We become exhausted, depleted by the pressure and effort that change requires. Before long, progress slows or halts altogether

- We blame ourselves for failing and become angry and even more self-critical

Self-Criticism doesn't help you to move FORWARD. Compassion and ENCOURAGEMENT do. Be kind to YOURSELF.

Chapter 3

Is Your Critical Voice
Friend or Foe?

Vanessa's life looked as if it had turned around. A charismatic, caring woman who brightened the lives of her friends and family, she had made a habit of reminding herself how fortunate she was. Earlier in her life, Vanessa had been forced to live on welfare. Now that she was employed, she knew just how grateful she *should* be.

The problem was, Vanessa *really* hated her job—so much so that her entire mood changed every time she even thought about it. Unfortunately, the idea of applying for a different job didn't feel any easier.

Vanessa had always loved fashion and beauty, but couldn't imagine herself getting her dream job in that industry. In fact, the mere thought of pursuing her dream always caused her critical voice to rear its ugly head. Each time, she'd tell herself the same "stuck story" she'd been carrying around for years:

I should be grateful for the job I have now because I'm not pretty enough or qualified enough to do what I love. One day I'll be able to make a change, but not yet.

Whenever Vanessa thought about making a career change, she'd hear her critical voice and her heart would race. Her anxiety was overwhelming. This strong physical reaction validated what her critical voice was saying. It always felt as if her body was telling her that her critical voice was correct—that she *shouldn't* apply for a job she wanted; that she *wasn't* good enough to go for it. Vanessa would then get quiet and shrink and remind herself that she *should* be grateful to have a job at all.

During one of my online courses, Vanessa heard me speak about the power of Tapping on the critical voice. She decided to try it and tapped on what her critical voice often said to her about her career. She soon realized that her critical voice had misled her; pursuing her dream *was* worthwhile. Even if she didn't get the job, she'd feel proud of herself for trying. After tapping, instead of feeling terrified of rejection, she felt ready and willing to give her dream career a try.

One day Vanessa surprised herself by walking into her favorite cosmetics store with her resume in hand. After asking for the manager, she shared her passion for beauty and her desire to work there. Within a matter of minutes, the manager invited her back for an interview. Suddenly, her dream career felt possible, all because she'd used Tapping to create a healthier relationship with her critical voice.

Do you tell yourself you're "not good enough" to go for your dreams? Have you ever delayed your own enjoyment or deprived yourself of pleasure because of things you believe are "wrong" with you or your life? Do you do it often?

In at least one area, and probably several areas, of our lives, many of us have spent years trying to hate ourselves happy. Instead of seeing what is possible, we make our own happiness contingent upon meeting goals. We tell ourselves that we can't relax until we pay off all of our debt or get a new job; that we can't feel good about ourselves until we find love or get in shape.

Let's be honest, though. If hating yourself happy worked, you, I, Vanessa, and millions of others would be living in a state of perpetual ecstasy. We would have hated ourselves happy years ago!

The real truth is that our critical voice doesn't make us happy or help us get unstuck. Instead, it keeps us cycling through the pattern of panic, *dis*connected from our flow and our joy and *un*able to make positive changes that last.

Now that you've begun to notice how your own pattern of panic looks and feels, we're going to look at the role that your critical voice plays in keeping you in that pattern. Using Tapping, we'll then begin to quiet the critical voice and, in the process, finally break free from the panic.

Hard Fact or Convincing Fiction?

When we have a belief about ourselves, our lives, even what we have to sacrifice in order to create positive change, we unconsciously act in congruence with that belief. If you feel that you aren't good enough, your primitive brain will search for evidence to prove that belief. Conversely, if you believe that you are good enough, your mind will search for all the evidence that proves *that* belief.

Beliefs are tricky like that. Once we're sure of them, our brains find evidence to back them up.

Negative beliefs also create a strong emotional response in the body (pressure in our chest, a pain in our stomach), which reinforces the idea that the belief we hold must be true. We're then more likely to feel defeated, which causes us to fall back into the pattern of panic.

This cycle quickly becomes self-perpetuating. Over time, our inability to break out of our pattern of panic reinforces (yet again) the illusion that our limiting beliefs are truths, rather than beliefs. As time goes on, we become even more attached to our critical voice, rather than less.

What we overlook in this process is the fact that the critical voice is the voice of the primitive brain. It's our fear being broadcast through an internal loudspeaker, doing everything it can to keep us safe.

As we've learned, the primitive brain equates staying safe with avoiding change, even when that change is good for us. That's because change is uncertain and unpredictable, and the primitive brain prefers safety and certainty.

So if the critical voice is hurting us and holding us back, why do we hold on to it?

Shattering the Illusion of Success

"But it *works*!"

That's one of the objections I hear often when I teach a class about quieting the critical voice. Like many of my clients, I used to pride myself on how hard and critical I was on myself. I thought it made me an intelligent and self-aware person.

It's a commonly held belief. Over and over again, clients tell me that they'd never lose weight or apply for that job or start dating if their critical voice wasn't riding them.

"Okay," I respond, "but when your critical voice is screaming at you to make a change, is that change sustainable, or do your efforts produce temporary results?"

Almost without exception, the changes we make as a result of our critical voice don't last. That's because they're coming from a place of panic.

Let's also be honest about something—the critical voice is exhausting! It's a ruthless taskmaster, always demanding more, better, faster. As a result, the process of moving toward our goals and desires doesn't feel enjoyable. Instead it feels harsh and limiting. As time goes on, we get tired. We feel worn down, so we do what we know how to do best—we return to our old, self-sabotaging ways. Then the pattern of panic starts all over again.

Inner Critic or Inner Bully?

Imagine yourself standing in front of a young child who's scared. Now picture yourself yelling at that scared little child, telling her she's being stupid, and she shouldn't feel that way. In response to your insults, she cries even louder, which prompts you to yell more, saying things like "Just get over it! You never do anything right." Finally, you've had enough. You turn around and walk away, leaving the traumatized child all alone.

Can you picture yourself actually doing that—yelling at a scared child and then abandoning her? Of course not! We hear that story and immediately and think, *I would* never *be so cruel to a child.* Yet without noticing, we let our critical voice be exactly that harsh and heartless to our own selves. When we are feeling scared to take action, or when we are struggling with an emotion like disappointment, we need our own love and support the most, but it's often in those moments that we abandon ourselves.

Think about it . . . what do you say to yourself when you make a mistake? What do you tell yourself when you do something that embarrasses you? If you're like most people I've worked with, you tell yourself that you're dumb, clumsy, or not smart; that you're not good enough, not qualified enough, not attractive enough—and more.

You repeatedly say things to yourself that you would never say to a scared little child! You say things that you'd never say to a friend or loved one. You do it again and again, and over time your critical voice becomes your inner bully.

To be clear, we don't intend to be mean to ourselves. We let this happen because it's what our culture has taught us. Since childhood, we've been taught to strive and excel, to "do better" and "be better," but very rarely are we taught that we're enough just as we are.

Is the Critical Voice All Bad?

So is the critical voice all bad? Aren't there times when we need to hear those harsh truths we'd avoid otherwise?

One of my favorite perspectives on the role of the critical voice comes from Iyanla Vanzant. As the author of six *New York Times* best-selling books and executive producer and host of *Iyanla: Fix My Life* television show, she has spent a lot of time in the public eye.

One day while I was interviewing her, I asked her about her own critical voice. Iyanla shared that after years of struggling with it, she realized that her critical voice was giving her a false sense of control. Her primitive brain reasoned that if she was always the first person to point out her faults and imperfections, she wouldn't be hurt when others did. Basically, her inner critic had become a kind of inner armor, a shield intended for self-defense.

Once she realized that, she knew that what her critical voice was craving wasn't more fuel for self-critique. Instead, it needed more comfort and reassurance. To meet those needs, she now uses self-care and self-love as ways of preventing her critical voice from becoming too powerful. By prioritizing self-care, she's able to meet these needs better. As a result, her critical voice doesn't need to become an inner bully.

Iyanla was quick to point out that self-care and self-love don't completely silence her critical voice. However, now that she's taking better care of herself, her critical voice doesn't have as much power. When it points out mistakes or missteps, she can hear its message with an open mind, and without feeling shame or self-loathing.

Rather than rendering her critical voice all-powerful or completely powerless, she treats it like a well-intentioned friend whose opinion she can agree with—or not.

We all have a voice inside that tells us we aren't good enough.
We don't need to heal, fix, or fight this voice. Simply acknowledge
that the voice appears when we are scared, and it's when we
need our own love and reassurance the most.

From Inner Bully to Inner Ally

Weeks after the course, Vanessa reached out to me and shared that she'd been offered the job. Her dream career was about to begin, all because she'd used Tapping to quiet her critical voice.

Rather than continuing to hate herself happy, which for her looked like force-feeding herself gratitude for a job she hated, she had gained clarity and found her flow by quieting her critical voice. Her critical voice hadn't made her feel more grateful; it had prevented her from realizing her desires.

These beliefs about our need for our critical voice aren't always conscious. Sometimes our reliance on the critical voice may even seem helpful, as if we're tempting ourselves with a future reward. However, skimping on joy while we move toward our desires quickly becomes self-defeating. That's because as soon as we achieve one goal, we find a new one standing between us and our flow, us and our joy. Regardless of how many goals we achieve, when we're holding on to our critical voice, we never have permission to feel joy or be in our flow. Instead of moving forward, we inevitably stay stuck.

Using Tapping, we can begin to open up to ways of turning the critical voice from our inner bully into our inner ally. It's a gradual process. Like Iyanla, Vanessa didn't completely silence her critical voice, but she was able to quiet it enough to take one positive action step. That's a great example of how we can slowly but surely use Tapping to accept and better care for ourselves.

What Is Your Critical Voice Saying?

Without thinking too much about it, check off some of the things your critical voice says to you when you're in a state of panic, whether that panic is a mild, underlying anxiety or tension or a more noticeable, frantic feeling.

When I make a mistake or things aren't working, my critical voice says . . .

____ I'm not [smart, talented, good] enough.

____ I'm too [fat, old, skinny, young].

____ I never stick to anything.

____ If I don't criticize myself, I'll never change.

My critical voice also says . . .

_____

_____

_____

Read through your list. Now ask yourself, Would I say these things to a frightened child? To a friend or loved one?

Next we'll look at how your critical voice makes you feel.

Noticing Your *Emotional* Response

When you read through your list of the things your critical voice says to you, how do you feel? Do you feel peaceful, empowered, and confident? Probably not! Most of us feel anxious, stressed, even hopeless, frustrated, and angry when our critical voice is screaming at us.

Again without thinking too much about it, complete these sentences:

When my critical voice is saying harsh things to me, I feel . . .

___ Afraid that my critical voice is right

___ Angry at myself for not being able to overcome this by now

___ Frustrated that I'm *still* [in debt, this size, alone, fill in the blank]

___ Ashamed of myself or my life

___ Sad that I'm [X number of] years old and still stuck in this way

Fill in any other emotions you feel in response to your critical voice:

_____

_____

_____

When we stop and notice which emotions we feel in response to our critical voice, most of us get very clear on how closely linked our critical voice is to our pattern of panic. After all, if your critical voice was actually supporting you in moving toward your desires, it wouldn't cause you to feel anxious, frustrated, resentful, angry, or stressed. More likely it would make you feel excited and energized, with maybe just a hint of nervousness.

Next we'll look at how Tapping supports us in creating a healthier relationship with our critical voice.

Relaxed Body, Quieter Mind

When we use Tapping while focusing on the negative beliefs that the critical voice is offering us, we relax the body, which sends a calming signal to the primitive brain. The physical relaxation we experience tells the primitive brain that we're safe, even when we're thinking harsh thoughts about ourselves (*You're not good enough*, *You should be further along by now*, and so on).

At that point, we're not as easily triggered by our critical voice, so the negative thoughts it sends us don't throw us into the pattern of panic. Instead, thanks to Tapping, we're able to step back and see that what the critical voice is saying isn't true. We then realize that the critical voice is just the scared child inside us, is trying to keep us safe.

When we have an idea, a vision of what we want, we create a spark inside ourselves. When that vision doesn't materialize in the physical world fast enough, too often we let our critical voice throw a damp blanket on that inner spark. To manifest that desire, we need to nurture the spark, not deprive it of oxygen through judgment and criticism.

Keep in mind that we never fully get rid of our critical voice. Our goal is to honor the positive intention behind that voice (to keep you safe) while realizing that it is safe for you to get unstuck, even as you navigate the uncertainty involved in creating change.

Quieting Your Critical Voice

Let's do some Tapping now on quieting your critical voice.

Looking back at your list of negative beliefs that your critical voice says to you, pick the one belief that feels most true at this moment.

Rate how true that particular belief feels on a scale of 0 to 10, with 10 being completely true.

Take a deep breath.

We'll begin by tapping on the Karate Chop point.

Note: This is a sample Tapping script, with only one negative round and one positive. The complete, expanded script is in the Appendix on page 193.

Karate Chop *(repeat three times)*: Even though I've been holding on to this belief, I accept how I feel and choose to relax.

Sample Negative Round:

Eyebrow: This belief

Side of Eye: It feels so true

Under Eye: I've had this belief for a long time

Under Nose: <State your belief now>

Under Mouth: It's a story I keep telling myself

Collarbone: To try to protect myself from disappointment

Under Arm: Right now this feels true to me

Top of Head: And that's okay

Sample Positive Round:

Eyebrow: I feel safe questioning my beliefs

Side of Eye: As I relax my mind

Under Eye: And feel centered in my body

Under Nose: I can ask myself

Under Mouth: Is this really true?

Collarbone: I don't have to believe

Under Arm: Everything I think

Top of Head: I reexamine what feels true to me

Take a deep breath. When you think about what your critical voice is saying to you, how true does it feel now? Give it a number on a scale of 0 to 10.

Keep tapping until you can have the thought without feeling anxiety or panic in any form. At that point it will no longer feel true.

Now that we've begun to relax and disconnect from the pattern of panic and our critical voice, in the next chapter we'll look at how to navigate the fear and uncertainty that can keep us stuck.

Time for the End-of-Chapter Tapping Meditation!

It's time to use the Tapping Meditation to begin quieting the pattern of panic. Before moving on to the next chapter, tap through the Chapter 3 Tapping Meditation.

If you're new to Tapping, first refer to the Quick Start Tapping Guide starting on page xix.

CHAPTER 3 TAPPING MEDITATION: QUIETING YOUR CRITICAL VOICE

Close your eyes and focus your attention on what your critical voice says to you most often. As you do that, mentally scan your body. Notice any sensations you feel. These are ways that your body is reacting to your critical voice.

Focus on the primary one or two emotions you feel most intensely in response to your critical voice. Rate the intensity of that emotion on a scale of 0 to 10, with 10 being the highest intensity you can imagine.

With your primary emotion(s) in mind, let's start tapping.

As you tap through the rounds, feel free to substitute words that reflect your experience. Also be aware of how your experience shifts during and after Tapping.

Take a deep breath.

Begin tapping on the Karate Chop point.

Karate Chop *(repeat three times)*: Even though my critical voice is saying these harsh things to me, I accept myself and choose to relax now.

Eyebrow: I'm so hard on myself

Side of Eye: My critical voice

Under Eye: It's always there

Under Nose: Ready to bring me down

Under Mouth: These things I say to myself

Collarbone: I'd never say them to a scared child

Under Arm: I'd never say them to a loved one

Top of Head: I'm so hard on myself

Eyebrow: I've been self-critical for so long

Side of Eye: And part of me doesn't think I can change

Under Eye: Part of me listens to this voice

Under Nose: Because I think it'll help

Under Mouth: I've been trying to hate myself happy

Collarbone: I've been trying to criticize myself to change

Under Arm: I acknowledge the pain this has caused me

Top of Head: And how stuck I feel

Eyebrow: I acknowledge my critical voice

Side of Eye: And all the anxiety that comes with it

Under Eye: All this self-criticism

Under Nose: It's hard to live with

Under Mouth: It makes me anxious

Collarbone: It makes me panic

Under Arm: I'm tired of fighting my critical voice

Top of Head: I'm open to a new way

Eyebrow: I begin to notice when I hear my critical voice

Side of Eye: I notice how I feel

Under Eye: Am I scared or overwhelmed?

Under Nose: I acknowledge the emotions behind this voice

Under Mouth: I honor my feelings

Collarbone: I honor how hard this has been

Under Arm: I don't need to fight my critical voice

Top of Head: I simply honor how I feel

Eyebrow: I allow my body to relax

Side of Eye: This critical voice is simply an invitation

Under Eye: To practice kindness and self-compassion

Under Nose: I release the need to fight it

Under Mouth: I remember that I am safe

Collarbone: I don't need to believe

Under Arm: Everything that I think

Top of Head: I give my body permission to relax

Eyebrow: As I feel centered in my body

Side of Eye: I choose to be a good friend to myself

Under Eye: I have my own back

Under Nose: I nurture my spirit with positive thoughts

Under Mouth: I am in control of what I focus on

Collarbone: I focus on my gifts

Under Arm: I have so much to share with this world

Top of Head: I clear my path with encouraging thoughts

Take a deep breath. Check back in with yourself, notice the intensity of your panic response now, and rate it again on a scale of 0 to 10.

Chapter 4

Navigating through Fear and Uncertainty

We all go through times in our lives when we feel frozen, stalled in one part (or several parts) of our lives. That "stuck" experience can manifest as emotional numbness, overwhelming anxiety, or a mix of both—and more! However being stuck manifests at a given time, we're almost always aware of a need to create change in order to get unstuck. Since change involves uncertainty, and uncertainty prompts the primitive brain to create fear, creating the change we know we need feels hard.

In this chapter we'll look at how and why our fear of the unknown keeps us stuck, and use Tapping to move through it with greater ease.

Why Uncertainty and Fear Take Hold

When we get stuck in our fear of uncertainty, taking action and creating movement can seem impossible. We've already looked at one reason that fear can be so paralyzing—because it's ingrained in our survival instinct (the primitive brain's specialty) and reinforced in the body. Another important reason that fear takes hold of us is because of where it's rooted—in our beliefs.

Beliefs are sneaky. They're those ideas we take for granted, the basic understandings we accept as "truth." In order to see limiting beliefs as what they actually are—ideas that are keeping us stuck—we need to tap through the fear they create. Once we lessen the intensity of our fear, we can objectively consider whether our limiting beliefs are actually true. Once we realize that they are just beliefs, not the truth, we're free to take on new and more empowering beliefs that support us in finding our flow.

Before we explore some common limiting beliefs that keep us stuck in our fear of uncertainty, let's take a deep breath and remember that there's no shame in having limiting beliefs. It's normal to have them. We all have some! These limiting beliefs were created with good intentions; they were our way to keep ourselves safe, and as children they may have worked wonderfully. If you were criticized every time you made a mistake, then the belief you need to play small and not speak up was helpful because it prevented conflict. As an adult with more resources and understanding, that same belief limits you and causes pain.

Let's not label ourselves as "messed up" or "damaged" because we have limiting beliefs. Our goal here is to get curious, not critical. Let's get interested in what's keeping us stuck. We can then use Tapping to release what's no longer serving us, all while being kinder and gentler with ourselves than we've ever been.

Are you ready? Let's look at commonly held beliefs that keep us stuck in our fear of uncertainty.

Belief #1: "I need all the answers before I can move forward."

When we know what we want but don't know how to get it, we often end up feeling stuck. This progression makes perfect sense given that the primitive brain is wired for certainty and safety. When we think we know what's coming, we at least feel like we're in control. When we're aware of how much uncertainty we're dealing with, however, we're a lot more likely to get lost in worry about everything we don't know. We think, *What if this happens? What if that happens?* Uncertainty can feel really scary!

Because of that fear of the unknown, we may act like a deer in headlights. Rather than getting curious about what's next, we freeze in the face of everything that we don't know. We get stuck in fear.

The fear we feel around not having the answers may also be intensified by our cultural belief that making mistakes isn't okay. If we don't get it "right" the first time, we've been taught to blame and shame ourselves, instead of simply course-correcting and trying again.

I had these experiences when my brother, his friend Nick Polizzi, and I began making the documentary film *The Tapping Solution*. It was a long journey that we started with more questions than answers. How do we get the film equipment? How do we learn about lighting? How do we convince experts to give us interviews? How do we edit? How do we distribute the film? How can this film help the most people?

The uncertainty often felt overwhelming, and without Tapping, our list of unanswered questions would have felt paralyzing. Eventually we realized that if we waited until we had all the necessary answers, we would never get started. Instead, we focused on one challenge at a time and relied on trial and error to move forward. It wasn't easy. None of the footage we filmed in the first six months turned out to be usable. However, during those months, by gaining clarity on what wasn't working, we also gained clarity on what did work. Every trial and every error eventually led us to the answers we needed. It was through taking imperfect action that we gained the clarity we needed to move forward.

Harnessing the Power of Mistakes

Arianna Huffington, co-founder of *The Huffington Post*, grew up in a small one-bedroom apartment with her mother and sister. During an interview I did with her, Arianna shared that her mother used to tell her something that still guides her today:

"Failure is not the opposite of success; it's part of it."

Every successful person I've ever known, interviewed, or researched has experienced more failure than success. Even after achieving enormous success, they continue to fail. Over time, they learn to embrace the ups and downs that come with success. Rather than feeling threatened by failure, they get curious. As appealing as this mind-set may seem, it's not easy to embrace. The fear of failure is deeply ingrained in the primitive brain.

I often wonder if we shouldn't let go of the word *failure* altogether. It's such a silly word that holds so much emotional weight. You didn't fail; you had expectations that weren't met, and you feel disappointed. You label that experience as "failure" when someone else might view it as information, a stepping-stone to something better. As Thomas Edison is believed to have said about his time working on the lightbulb, "I haven't failed, I've just found 10,000 ways that won't work."

Rather than treating disappointments as failures, rather than judging unmet expectations as verdicts on our abilities or potential, we can begin to view disappointing experiences as scientists do—as data points. When scientists conduct experiments, they don't hide the experiments that produce unexpected, even undesired, results; they record, study, and analyze them. They use those "failures" as guides. They relate to their failures as they relate to a teacher who can and will bring them one step closer to their desired outcome.

> *"Ideas don't come out fully formed. They only become clear as you work on them. You just have to get started."*
>
> — Mark Zuckerberg, CEO of Facebook

Keep in mind, this journey definitely isn't about pushing more. Nor is it about forcing things. It's not even about becoming fearless. Instead, we can use Tapping to fear less. From that place we're better able to hear our intuition and gain clarity.

Activating Your Internal GPS

> *Faith is taking the first step even when you don't see the whole staircase.*
>
> — Martin Luther King, Jr.

My friend Mike Dooley, author of *Notes from the Universe*, shares a metaphor that's incredibly helpful when we're talking about moving past our fear of the unknown.

He talks about the GPS navigation system in a car. If you get into the car and leave it in "park," the GPS does nothing for you. It can't help you. However, the moment you turn the car on and it starts moving, your GPS becomes your ally. It tells you when to turn, when to go straight, exit, and even when to make a legal U-turn. It guides you, but only after you take that first step and get the car moving.

That same idea applies to creating change. You have to take action—even when you're scared of everything you don't know, even when you don't have all the answers. You have to move in order for your own intuition and the Universe to support and guide you. If you stay in "park" because you don't know every mile you may travel, you stay stuck, unable to access the help you'd otherwise receive.

Every one of the best things in my life has been the result of movement and magic. However, that magic only became available *after* I did something (or many things!) to create movement in my life.

Even when you make wrong turns, those missteps can and will steer you in a better, more fruitful direction. You've made U-turns in your car, and there will be times when you need to make them in your life. The only way to course-correct, though, is to create movement. You have to be in motion for your inner wisdom and the Universe to lend a hand.

By letting fear of uncertainty prevent us from moving forward, we also rob ourselves of the chance to discover a different path or direction based on the new information that we receive.

Action, even imperfect action, leads us back into flow. That's because action breeds clarity. Making a course correction as we move forward *is* progress.

This same principle applies to what I call "future-tripping." When we stay stuck because we're trying to solve problems that don't yet exist, we're magnifying our fear of the unknown rather than releasing it.

In a culture that values extremes, we often forget that taking action and creating change often happens in incremental, everyday ways. Simple actions like doing 10 minutes of research, asking a new question, reaching out to a certain person or group of people—all of these count as action steps. It's through taking these seemingly small action steps day after day, week after week that we create the change we long for.

Let's do some Tapping on feeling safe taking action even though you don't know where that action will lead you, and even though you'll eventually face problems that you don't yet know how to solve. This is the first step to activating, and trusting, your internal GPS.

To begin, rate how much fear you feel when you think about taking action when you don't know the outcome. Give it a number on a scale of 0 to 10.

Note: This is a sample Tapping script, with only one negative round and one positive. The complete, expanded script is in the Appendix on page 195.

Take a deep breath.

We'll begin by tapping on the Karate Chop point.

Karate Chop *(repeat three times)*: Even though I feel all this fear around taking action when I don't know how things will turn out, I choose to relax and feel peace now.

Sample Negative Round:

Eyebrow: All this fear

Side of Eye: I can feel it in my body

Under Eye: I want to take a step forward

Under Nose: But I feel frozen

Under Mouth: I'm unsure of what to do

Collarbone: I don't know what will work

Under Arm: I'm afraid

Top of Head: I feel stuck in place

Sample Positive Round:

Eyebrow: I acknowledge my fear

Side of Eye: And relax my body

Under Eye: Even without all the answers

Under Nose: I can feel centered and calm

Under Mouth: I am being guided

Collarbone: I am open to my intuition

Under Arm: It's safe to take action

Top of Head: I'm safe moving forward

Take a deep breath. On a scale of 0 to 10, once again rate the intensity of your fear of creating movement even when the results are unknown. Rather than trying to tap away all of your fear, continue tapping until you simply feel willing to take action in spite of your fear. That's huge progress!

Belief #2: "I have to heal completely; then I can move forward."

I was reminded of how paralyzing this belief can be during an event I was co-leading with my friend Erin Stutland, a coach and fitness expert. We were talking about feeling stuck when a woman raised her hand. She explained that she's long held a belief that she's not good enough. For years she'd taken workshops, read books, done therapy, and reached out to practitioners of different techniques and modalities. She felt she needed to rid herself of that belief. Every time that belief crept back in, she felt it meant that she had failed.

Erin and I both looked at her with compassion, seeing the pressure she was putting on herself. We then looked at each other, knowing that we were thinking the same thing. "Welcome to the club!" we both wanted to shout. The truth is, most of have limiting beliefs like *I'm not good enough*. That's okay! In fact, it's not even a problem.

It's a place most of us go to when we are feeling scared, uncertain, and vulnerable.

To get unstuck, we don't have to banish that belief forever. If we put that expectation between us and the change we desire, we resort to the pattern of panic, telling ourselves we need total healing and perfect beliefs in order to get unstuck.

The reality is, when you're feeling vulnerable, maybe because you're scared or simply didn't have a good night's sleep, the voice that says "I'm not good enough" may reappear. It is part of the critical voice, which we can never completely get rid of. Instead we begin to understand that we don't have to believe every thought we have.

Tapping supports this process by lessening the intensity of the fear we feel as a result of our limiting beliefs. When we tap, we can lower the intensity enough to take a step back and ask ourselves, *Am I really not good enough, or am I just scared?* When we are able to address how we are feeling, we can tap and release the fear in order to give ourselves the love and reassurance we crave.

Rather than seeking total healing, we only need to seek relief and ease. We don't need perfect beliefs or perfect emotions. We can simply use Tapping to release some of the negative emotional charge behind our limiting beliefs. Since Tapping calms the nervous system, we can then reconnect with our own creativity, love, and problem-solving abilities. Most importantly, by focusing on getting relief, we allow ourselves to feel self-compassion and self-acceptance.

As you think about Tapping and any inner work you're doing, ask yourself:

How can I give myself a little relief? How can I create more ease when I feel stuck?

If you feel like relief and ease aren't enough, notice that story. Do some Tapping as you tell yourself that story around needing "total healing" to get unstuck. See what shifts as you tap through it.

It's Always the Perfect Time

Few people have embodied the idea that healing happens in layers better than Louise Hay. I was honored to witness a small but powerful piece of her journey years ago. I was watching my brother interview her on camera for our yearly event, The Tapping World Summit. At the time, Louise was 87. During the interview, she shared that there were childhood issues that she was feeling called to release.

I remember feeling awe hearing her speak about it. This was a woman who had helped millions of people. She was often idolized in the personal development world, and there she was, openly sharing that she was still and always would be on a journey of greater healing. She didn't feel like anything was wrong or that she hadn't done enough inner work or healing. She wasn't blaming or shaming herself for being in her 80s and still needing to heal emotional wounds from childhood. Instead, she was allowing herself to move through the process when and how she felt called to.

Louise was moving through her self-discovery process with ease and self-compassion. It was never about reaching a final destination; it's simply part of the human experience.

Feeling and Healing Our Way Forward

Don't seek healing, just seek relief
Don't seek improvement, just seek relief
Don't seek solution, just seek relief
Just hold in your mind the idea of the stream that is
Flowing mightily toward all of the things that you want.

— Abraham-Hicks

Listening to Louise Hay that day, I realized how important it is for us to keep feeling and healing. We have to stop making ourselves wrong for feeling the wide range of emotions we inevitably feel. We have to stop punishing ourselves for being triggered *again* by that family member, friend, or childhood memory.

We have to stop blaming ourselves for feeling stuck and disconnected from our flow. Like Louise Hay, we need to give ourselves space and time to heal when and how we can.

We all have parts and places inside ourselves that need more love and compassion. That's normal, but also not a reason to stay stuck. By releasing the belief that we need to heal every deep wound first, we can relax into our flow more easily and quickly while also healing when and how it suits us.

From that place we can also see that we're already whole enough, good enough, strong enough, and lovable enough *exactly as we are*. We can commit to finding our flow without self-punishment, shame, or self-blame. We can acknowledge the parts of us that still feel unresolved, but not make healing those wounds into an obstacle standing in our way.

That's when we realize that moving forward into our flow isn't separate from healing our deeper wounds. Those experiences are interconnected, rather than sequential.

WHY EMPOWERING BELIEFS SOMETIMES DON'T "WORK"

Have you ever told yourself that you deserve abundance, but been unable to manage your money effectively? Have you ever repeated an affirmation that you deserve love and connection, but refused to start dating? Sometimes we take on new, empowering beliefs, but struggle to transform our actions and interactions in the world. It's frustrating!

That happens when we take on new beliefs that we believe . . . but only sort of. As much as we want to rush and force-feed ourselves new and empowering beliefs, since we heal in layers, the process can take time. If you find that your new, empowering beliefs aren't reflected in your actions and reactions, take some time to be honest with yourself about any doubts and fears you still harbor about them. Tap on how you're actually feeling until those negative emotions feel less intense. Don't be surprised if it takes repeated Tapping to lessen the intensity of your fears and doubts. You don't have to tap through every last bit of negative emotion for your new, positive beliefs to support you in finding your flow. Just keep tapping on how you honestly feel, letting yourself release those emotions little by little, and layer by layer. You've got this!

To Grow, We Must Stretch

While being stuck is unfulfilling and often frustrating, the primitive brain knows something we may forget—being stuck is safer than creating the movement necessary to create change.

When we hold on to the belief that we have to banish every fear and insecurity and feel completely confident and clear before creating change, we may also be avoiding the fear and discomfort we feel around putting ourselves out there. Instead of moving ahead, we tell ourselves that we need to withdraw and focus on self-improvement.

Although inner work may be challenging and uncomfortable, it also allows us to stay somewhat hidden. It protects us from the risk of shining our light in the world, and potentially being ridiculed or rejected as a result. Obsessing about having perfect emotions and beliefs or a perfect spiritual practice is another way of holding ourselves back. It's another way we keep ourselves stuck and avoid creating the lasting change we desire.

The truth is, every time we do something new and expand, every time we grow, we inevitably experience discomfort. To grow, we must stretch, and stretching doesn't always feel perfect. The discomfort and fear it brings up are normal parts of the change process. They're not reasons to stop taking action or to retreat exclusively into our inner work. Instead, they're a call to notice how we're feeling, to work on processing and releasing it *as* we continue creating movement in our life.

Ask yourself:

Do I tell myself that one day I'll be able to make a change, after I work on myself enough that I clear every single doubt or insecurity?

Next, notice how strongly the belief *I have to heal completely before I can find my flow* feels. Give it a number on a scale of 0 to 10.

Note: This is a sample Tapping script, with only one negative round and one positive. The complete, expanded script is in the Appendix on page 198.

Take a deep breath.

We'll begin by tapping on the Karate Chop point.

Karate Chop *(repeat three times)*: Even though I still have doubts, I honor how I feel and give myself permission to experiment.

Sample Negative Round:

Eyebrow: Part of me is ready to take action

Side of Eye: But sometimes I still have doubts

Under Eye: I'm waiting for the perfect moment

Under Nose: I keep blaming myself

Under Mouth: I try to clear every doubt

Collarbone: I try to clear every insecurity

Under Arm: And I just feel more stuck

Top of Head: All this pressure I put on myself

Sample Positive Round:

Eyebrow: I can be really ready

Side of Eye: And still a little scared

Under Eye: I can move forward

Under Nose: Even when it feels new and uncomfortable

Under Mouth: It's safe to experiment

Collarbone: I honor my feelings

Under Arm: I give myself the reassurance I crave

Top of Head: Now is my time

Take a deep breath. Check back in with yourself and again rate how true this belief feels on a scale of 0 to 10. Keep tapping on releasing your belief and letting yourself feel the deeper emotions behind it, such as fear of having to put yourself out there.

Belief #3: *"I will relax and find my flow when I achieve <this goal>."*

During an event one day, Ali raised her hand to share her "stuck" story. She'd wanted to leave her job for a long time. The good news was, she'd recently applied for a new job that she was excited about. She'd been thrilled to land an interview. It was scheduled for the following week, now just three days away.

When I asked Ali how she was stuck, she said, "Well, I just don't know if it will all work out."

I nodded and explained that she wasn't actually stuck. She was wrestling with the uncertainty that's ever present in our lives. Because she felt paralyzed by her fear of the unknown, she'd put her goal of getting a new job between her and finding flow.

All Ali needed to do was tap on her fear and remind herself about the power of patience. She'd been putting so much time and energy into this one part of her life that she'd begun expecting the Universe to deliver what she wanted exactly when and how she wanted it.

It's another way we fall into future-tripping. It tends to happen when we work so hard at moving our lives forward that we naturally want what we want when and how we want it! There's no shame in that, but to find our flow, we also need to let ourselves relax. We have to remember that being patient and enjoying the ride along the way allows the Universe to support us in its own way and according to its own divine timing. It's easier said than done, which is another reason I'm grateful for Tapping!

The Power of Just Being

After doing some Tapping on her fear of uncertainty, Ali realized that she was already in her flow. She was taking action, even though she still felt afraid. Her fear was still there, but it was no longer so overwhelming that it paralyzed her.

Her story was a great reminder that along the way to realizing our dreams and creating movement, we have to celebrate the small wins, rather than placing all of the emphasis on the big ones. If we put our joy and flow on hold because of a goal we haven't yet achieved, we miss the opportunity to enjoy the other abundance that's already present in our lives and savor our progress.

Are you putting your flow on hold because of one (or several) dreams you haven't yet realized?

On a scale of 0 to 10, rate how true this statement feels: *I can't find my flow or my joy until I've* <state your goal here>.

Note: This is a sample Tapping script, with only one negative round and one positive. The complete, expanded script is in the Appendix on page 200.

Take a deep breath.

We'll begin by tapping on the Karate Chop point.

Karate Chop *(repeat three times)*: Even though I feel like I can't enjoy my progress until I reach my goal, I honor how I feel and I'm open to a new way.

Sample Negative Round:

Eyebrow: This goal

Side of Eye: I have to achieve it first

Under Eye: I have to push to get there

Under Nose: I feel like I can't relax until I've done that

Under Mouth: I honor how exhausting it is

Collarbone: To always feel like I need to do more

Under Arm: Without honoring all I've done

Top of Head: All this pressure I put on myself

Sample Positive Round:

Eyebrow: I honor every step forward

Side of Eye: I celebrate every little success

Under Eye: When I find joy within the process

Under Nose: It's easier to take the next step

Under Mouth: I can still desire more

Collarbone: And feel good about where I am

Under Arm: I can relax in this moment

Top of Head: And still dream about the future

Take a deep breath.

Again rate how true your belief that you have to realize your goal first feels on a scale of 0 to 10. Keep tapping until that belief is overshadowed by a willingness to find your flow first, before realizing that goal or dream.

THE LIFE PURPOSE TRAP

I often see a similar pattern play out around the idea of life purpose. When we feel like we need one big life purpose, we can get stuck in the pattern of panic with our critical voice blaming us for not figuring "it" out yet.

Let's face it, though, trying to pinpoint our *one* and *only* life purpose is a big task. It's also stressful! It's such a significant distraction that it can also become *the* reason that we don't try new things, learn new skills, or put ourselves out there and risk feeling disappointed or rejected. After all, if it's not our life purpose, why bother?

The pressure we feel to identify that single life purpose also prevents us from noticing that we can, and often do, experience a sense of purpose from multiple sources. We don't necessarily need one life purpose. Over time we may also find that our purpose and passions shift. What was motivating and fulfilling at 25 may not be when we're 45 or 60. That's a reflection of a natural cycle of change that occurs over time rather than the lack of a single life purpose.

Time for the End-of-Chapter Tapping Meditation!

Now that you've cleared some of the fear that has been keeping you stuck, make sure to use the Chapter 4 Tapping Meditation. In the next chapter, we'll continue to lay a foundation for the journey ahead by looking at how our physical surroundings impact our ability to create lasting change and find flow.

CHAPTER 4 TAPPING MEDITATION:
RELEASING THE FEAR OF MOVING FORWARD

When you think about taking action toward the change you desire, notice the intensity of your fear and rate it on a scale of 0 to 10.

As you tap through the rounds, feel free to substitute words that reflect your experience. Also be aware of how your experience shifts during and after tapping.

Take a deep breath.

We'll begin by tapping on the Karate Chop point.

Karate Chop *(repeat three times)*: Even though part of me believes that I need to have all the answers before I take a step forward, I honor how I feel and I'm open to seeing this in a new way.

Eyebrow: I know what I want

Side of Eye: Or at least I have an idea

Under Eye: But this desire feels overwhelming

Under Nose: I don't know how it's going to work out

Under Mouth: I think about it often

Collarbone: I worry about it

Under Arm: I have so many questions

Top of Head: And I have been searching for answers for so long

Eyebrow: All this worry

Side of Eye: All this uncertainty

Under Eye: All this anxiety

Under Nose: I can't feel better

Under Mouth: Until I have all the answers

Collarbone: I can't take action

Under Arm: Unless I know every step of the way

Top of Head: Is that really true?

Eyebrow: I have felt so stuck

Side of Eye: Waiting for the answers

Under Eye: One day I'll take action

Under Nose: But not until I'm certain this will work out

Under Mouth: Not until I have all the answers

Collarbone: But I've been waiting for so long

Under Arm: The more I think of it, the more stuck I feel

Top of Head: I am open to a new way

Eyebrow: I recognize the pressure I put on myself

Side of Eye: I thought I needed all the answers

Under Eye: I thought I needed to clear every insecurity

Under Nose: I thought I needed to do it perfectly

Under Mouth: No wonder it's been so hard to move forward

Collarbone: I honor how hard this has been

Under Arm: And I'm open to a new way

Top of Head: I give myself the reassurance and love I crave

Eyebrow: I honor the part of me that's hopeful

Side of Eye: I honor the part of me that feels excited

Under Eye: I also honor the part of me that's scared

Under Nose: There is room for all parts of me

Under Mouth: As I accept how I feel

Collarbone: I experience more ease

Under Arm: Maybe this can be easier than I thought?

Top of Head: Maybe I'm further along than I realize?

Eyebrow: I allow myself to get curious

Side of Eye: I give myself permission to experiment

Under Eye: It is safe to take this single step forward

Under Nose: Every step forward gives me clarity

Under Mouth: Clarity around what works and what doesn't

Collarbone: And that knowledge supports me

Under Arm: It's safe for me to experiment

Top of Head: It's safe for me to take action now

Take a deep, calming breath. Notice how intensely you feel fear around taking action now. Keep tapping until you feel the desired level of calm.

Chapter 5

Creating Space for Lasting Change and Flow

So far we've mostly looked at your internal environment—your beliefs and emotions. We'll continue that process later in the journey, but first, in the next three chapters we'll shift our focus to how your external environment can support you in creating lasting change. Using Tapping to add ease, we'll begin by first looking at two simple ways to create a physical environment that supports your desire to get unstuck and create lasting change.

Our home tells a story about who we are and how we feel. When we are feeling stuck in our life, that feeling begins to show up in our physical surroundings. We accumulate clutter and overlook disorder. Even our décor—the objects and colors we choose to surround ourselves with—may reflect how overwhelmed and uncertain we feel. When we're seeking ease, clarity, and flow as we create lasting change, it's important to create an environment that reflects those desires.

Stuff and Us

The first aspect of the external environment that we'll look at is clutter. Clutter, to me, is anything that you don't use, or don't need, or that doesn't bring you joy.

Over time, clutter goes from being a symptom of feeling stuck to contributing to the obstacles we're facing. Researchers at the Princeton Neuroscience Institute found that a cluttered environment limits our ability to focus. Their study, which looked at how people performed on a task in a cluttered versus uncluttered environment, demonstrated that physical clutter increases stress and diminishes performance.

Still to this day, one of my most powerful experiences with clutter happened when I was in high school. Growing up, we were an immigrant family living in a small town in Connecticut. My mom was a psychologist in the public school system, and my dad had his own business. While there was never much money, we always had what we needed.

By this point in my high school years, both of my brothers were off in college, and my dad's business had hit a rough patch. The environment at home felt tense and stressful, and I wasn't making my parents' lives any easier by complaining about our couch. It had big rips in it. My mom had tried to patch them, but it was clear that her brilliance as a psychologist didn't help her as a seamstress.

She was the first to admit that our couch wasn't pretty, but she reminded me that we didn't have money for a new couch, and it was the best she could do. I'm not proud to admit it, but I was so ashamed of our house that I stopped having friends over. I didn't want anyone to see our couch.

One day my mom noticed a book at our local library, *Clear Your Clutter with Feng Shui* by Karen Kingston, and checked it out. She stayed up late reading it and decided to implement some of the principles in our home, starting with removing clutter. When I came home from school that day, I wondered what had come over her. She was filling bags with items to donate.

Within a matter of days and without spending any money, my mom transformed our home. In the weeks that followed, people walked into our house and asked if we had bought new furniture or redecorated. I remember my brothers coming home during a college break and saying the house "felt" amazing and then jokingly complaining how unfair it was that the house became this nice after they had left.

More important, the stress and tension that had been so palpable in our home was replaced with a feeling of comfort and ease. Our home had become a sanctuary. My shame about our house, including our couch, quickly dissipated, and I once again began inviting friends over.

Soon afterward, something extraordinary happened. My dad's business began to turn around, and the money we needed began to flow again. I was amazed at how different our life had become—all from clearing clutter.

Could the timing of my dad's business turnaround have been a coincidence? Maybe. But also, without clutter overloading our senses, it's easier to think creatively. Without clutter it's also easier to focus and find things, both of which can increase productivity.

All of this is supported by research. In one study at UCLA, a team of researchers observed 32 mothers in Los Angeles. They found that the mothers' stress hormones, which restrict the brain's ability to focus and be creative, spiked when they were dealing with material possessions.

In my experience of that time and the many years since, I have found that there's a magic that happens when you clear clutter. It's not just about getting rid of stuff; it goes deeper than that. It impacts the brain, for sure, but also our emotional and spiritual well-being. By creating space in our physical environment, we create space for the change and flow we desire.

Feng Shui is the art of balancing and harmonizing the flow of natural energies in our surroundings to create beneficial effects in our lives.

— Karen Kingston

Hoarding Scarcity

Looking back, my mom's decluttering is especially inspiring given that she was brave enough to do it during a time of financial insecurity.

When we experience financial instability, it's often easier to fall into hoarding behaviors. That's because during those times we're most likely to fear that we won't have enough in the future. As a result, we hold on to things. We tell ourselves that we may need our current possessions in the future, and fear that we won't be able to afford replacing anything we get rid of now.

This way of thinking can become especially ingrained when we grow up poor or aware that money is in short supply. We may also experience comfort in holding on to things, believing that material possessions will help to fill the void we feel. If we're surrounded by things, we tell ourselves, we won't feel that gnawing sense of lack.

Sometimes we may also hold on to clutter because we think that gifts equal love, or that things keep our memories alive. During that week when my mom was decluttering our house, she donated a sad painting that her mother had given her. After reading about feng shui, my mom realized that the painting made her feel sad every time she looked at it. She'd only held on to it because it had been a gift from her mother.

Most of us fall into this pattern at one point or another. Especially once that person has passed away, getting rid of a keepsake may feel almost sacrilegious. However, in the absence of their gifts, will our memories of loved ones disappear? Of course not! Those who have had a profound impact on us stay with us, not just through our memories, but through the love and affection we've felt for them.

Although we may feel tempted to brush off this kind clutter as "just stuff," assuming it's no big deal to keep it, being surrounded by clutter, as we've seen, has a profound impact on how we feel and how we live. By donating that painting from her mom, my mom wasn't throwing away her love for her mother. She was giving herself more opportunities to feel good, which is a change she wanted to create. All these years later, my mom remembers her mother just as well as she did when she had that painting. The difference is that she doesn't get stuck in the unnecessary sadness she used to feel whenever she looked at that painting.

If you're struggling to let go of things, refer to the Chapter 5 Extended Tapping: Hoarding Scarcity on page 203 of the Appendix.

Common Clutter-Clearing Blocks

In her incredibly popular book *The Life-Changing Magic of Tidying Up*, Marie Kondo encourages readers to look at things and ask themselves, *Does this spark joy?* If the answer is no, donate it.

I love that idea. Being surrounded by things that truly spark joy is life changing. In that process, however, people sometimes run into blocks that hold them back and prevent them from clearing what is no longer serving them.

One common block people experience is this:

"But . . . I don't want to be wasteful."

I often hear this when I recommend getting rid of food that doesn't support health and wellness. The truth is that food will become waste either inside your body or outside your body. If food doesn't help your body thrive, letting it go to waste in the garbage is better than letting it turn into waste inside your stomach. Food waste is a problem that needs to be addressed, but consuming unhealthy food to avoid being wasteful does not solve that problem.

This same block can also come up around letting go of clothes. For instance, if you bought a sweater two years ago and you only wore it once, you might think, *Isn't it a waste of money to give it away?* The truth is it's a waste of energy (which impacts your money) to keep something that takes up space but doesn't bring joy. If you haven't been reaching for that sweater, there's probably a reason. Maybe it's itchy or maybe it doesn't feel right on your body. By donating that sweater, you are giving someone in need an opportunity to enjoy something that you don't. That is less wasteful than letting it sit in your closet unused. Most importantly, by releasing what doesn't serve you, you free up space and energy for the experiences you do wish to create.

Clearing *without* the Overwhelm

Abundance is a process of letting go; that which is empty can receive.
— Bryant H. McGill

In feng shui, clutter represents stagnant energy. The thinking is that we can't expect more in life if we don't have room for it. That is also one reason that many people's financial situations begin to improve when they clear clutter. There's room for more abundance in their lives.

Clutter is a weight that builds on top of us so gradually that most people don't even notice its effects. Once they do notice, the process of clearing it becomes so overwhelming that they do what they can to avoid it.

So where do we even start when it comes to clearing clutter?

Sorting and purging our stuff feels like more chores, more work, and too many decisions. People sometimes also feel embarrassed, even ashamed, and wonder, *How did I let it get this bad?* By tapping we can neutralize the experience, so we may not feel super excited to clear clutter at first, but we're at least willing. Once you start and notice how much better you feel, the process becomes even easier.

Let's do some Tapping on lessening that overwhelm now.

First think of a space—your home, office, car—that needs to be decluttered and notice how much overwhelm you feel when you think about doing it. Rate your overwhelm on a scale of 0 to 10.

Note: This is a sample Tapping script, with only one negative round and one positive. The complete, expanded script is in the Appendix on page 205.

Take a deep breath.

Begin tapping on the Karate Chop point.

Karate Chop *(repeat three times)*: Even though I feel so overwhelmed and ashamed when I even think about my clutter, I accept myself and how I feel.

Sample Negative Round:

Eyebrow: This clutter

Side of Eye: It's so overwhelming

Under Eye: How did I let it get so bad?

Under Nose: Clearing it is too much work

Under Mouth: This clutter

Collarbone: It's overwhelming

Under Arm: That's okay

Top of Head: I can let myself feel overwhelmed

Sample Positive Round:

Eyebrow: I can let go of this overwhelm around clearing clutter

Side of Eye: I can relax when I think about it

Under Eye: I can see it and release this shame

Under Nose: I can relax when I see this clutter

Under Mouth: And feel safe

Collarbone: Releasing this overwhelm now

Under Arm: Letting myself feel safe

Top of Head: I can relax when I think about clearing this clutter

Take a deep breath. Notice again how intense your overwhelm around clearing clutter feels, and give it a number of intensity on a scale of 0 to 10. Keep tapping until you experience the desired relief.

The Power of Pleasure

Another way to make the process of clearing clutter less overwhelming is to make it more pleasurable. Here are some of my favorite ways to do that:

- Lighting a favorite candle

- Playing inspiring and/or invigorating music

- Letting more sunshine in

- Listening to a favorite audiobook or podcast

- Sharing before and after pictures with friends who will cheer you on

- Repeating an affirmation as you clear (more on this next)

- Promising yourself a reward once you're done clearing a space

Motivation with Meaning

Once we feel less overwhelmed about eliminating clutter, it helps to assign meaning to the act of clearing it. I like to do this by focusing on an affirmation that feels empowering. As you clear clutter from an area, you can repeat it to yourself.

Affirmations turn the process of clearing into something bigger and deeper. They give meaning to a task that might otherwise feel tiresome or boring. As an example, if your first clearing project is your pantry, you might say to yourself:

As I clear out my pantry, I welcome new energy and improved wellness.

By using affirmations, you remind yourself that letting go of clutter is a way of ushering in the changes you desire.

Here are some of my favorite affirmations for clearing clutter:

Begin the sentence by naming the action:	End the sentence by infusing that action with symbolism:
As I clean out the cabinets in my kitchen . . .	. . . I usher in health and vitality.
As I put away the pile of shoes by the front door . . .	. . . I feel welcomed and comfortable in my home.
As I organize the bills in the drawer . . .	. . . I attract more opportunities and wealth.
As I let go of all the clothes that don't spark joy . . .	. . . I feel like I fit into my best life.
As I fix what's broken in my home . . .	. . . I feel whole and complete.
As I create a peaceful space in my bedroom . . .	. . . I easily feel relaxed and refreshed
As I let go of what I no longer need . . .	. . . I make room for miracles.
As I clear clutter from my car . . .	. . . I travel swiftly and comfortably toward my dreams.
As I clear the clutter in my home . . .	. . . I clear the clutter in my mind and gain more clarity.
As I let go of what reminds me of an old love . . .	. . . I open myself up to a new and greater love.

Feel free to mix and match and make your own affirmations!

TIPS FOR CLEARING CLUTTER AND KEEPING IT AWAY

- *Pick a small area to clear first.* By nature, clutter is overwhelming. By clearing a small space, you can more quickly celebrate your success. When you notice how good that accomplishment feels, continuing the process becomes exciting.

- *Save objects with sentimental value until the end.* By starting with the easier items in an area, we give ourselves the chance to feel more comfortable with letting go of clutter. At that point it feels easier to reflect on clutter that has sentimental value. Remember, if an item sparks joy, keep it. If it doesn't, thank the object for the memory. Choose to keep the memory and let go of the object. For additional support, use the *Chapter 5 Extended Tapping: Keeping the Memory and Letting Go of the Object* on page 208 of the Appendix.

- *Brag about your success!* Take before and after pictures of your cluttered area and send them to a friend who will cheer you on. My friend reorganized her drawers and sent me a picture that inspired me to do the same.

- *It's not about perfection.* Maintaining a home that has been decluttered isn't about keeping a space perfect all of the time. It's about living in an environment that feels good. If your kids are having fun making a mess, that's a happy mess that feels good and is temporary; enjoy the moment and don't worry that your home doesn't look perfect.

- *New habits keep clutter out.* Once you've decluttered a space, you may be tempted to resort to old habits. Whether it's keeping old clothes or letting mail pile up, when you notice yourself slipping, repeat the affirmation you used while decluttering and handle it right away.

Now that we've looked at the impact of clutter, it's time to consider another way that our physical surroundings may be keeping us stuck. Even once clutter has been cleared, the types of objects we surround ourselves with can have a significant impact.

The Story of Stuff

When I first met her, Charlotte was stuck in an on-again, off-again relationship that was coming to a slow and painful end. From the beginning, her relationship had been filled with drama, confusion, and passion. The uncertainty and unpredictability had kept her holding on, always hoping for more.

This pattern of getting stuck in unhealthy relationships was one that Charlotte had been running for years. She felt emotionally drained and knew that the relationship needed to end. Still, though, she struggled to let it go completely.

One day while taking my course, she looked at her bookshelves and noticed that all of her books were about heartbreaking romance. Every single day she was surrounded by intense, often painful love stories. She realized that she was living out the stories she was surrounding herself with. She then realized that she was ready for a new story, a new way to look at love and relationships. Determined to create a space that could support her new desire, Charlotte spent an evening gathering her books, and then donated them to her local library.

When I spoke to her next, she shared how surprised she was by the difference that letting go of those books had made; she hadn't felt this empowered in a very long time. Freed from the drama and pain of those love stories, she had also gained the courage to end her relationship. Getting rid of those books had allowed her to move toward the healthy relationship experience she wanted to create.

My friend Annalisa had a similar experience. Feeling stuck, she hired Ken Lauher, a feng shui expert, to help her create a more supportive living space. Although Ken knew nothing about Annalisa's personal life, he immediately noticed a painting of a large woman looking out into the distance, and in the opposite corner, a smaller man looking through a window. He asked Annalisa if she had a pattern of attracting men who were smaller (in passion, income, willingness to be emotionally involved, and so on). Annalisa was so dumbfounded, she wondered out loud if he was psychic; he'd pinpointed a central struggle she'd had in her life for some time.

Ken explained that we attract art and other objects that represent our current situation, even if our current situation isn't what we want. He often meets clients who feel lonely whose homes are decorated with paintings of lone figures in reflective, gloomy poses. These images and possessions continuously impact our subconscious, feeding into our "stuck" story, and preventing us from creating positive change. By changing our external environment to reflect a new story that we consciously choose and desire, we create an environment that supports the transformation we want to create.

Remember, your home tells a story, and you are the author! What story does your environment tell? Does it tell you a story that supports you in getting unstuck? Or is it reinforcing patterns that are keeping you stuck?

Focus your attention on one area of your home and notice the story it's telling. Then ask yourself, *Is this story supporting me in creating the change I desire, or is it keeping me stuck?* If a particular area feels neutral or empowering, move on to another area of your home until you find a story that isn't supportive. That's where your clearing should begin. As always, add affirmations and incorporate pleasure into the process.

Surrounding Yourself Happy

Once you've cleared clutter and gotten rid of things that are telling unhelpful stories, I highly recommend using some basic feng shui practices in your home. These simple, easy practices will help to create an environment that supports you in getting unstuck:

1. *Green up your space.* Bring nature inside by having live, beautiful plants. This not only freshens the air, it supports forward movement in your life. As they grow, you too transform and evolve!

2. *Make room for what you want.* Look at your space and ask yourself, *Does my space welcome what I desire?*

As an example, if you are looking for a relationship, make sure to have two pillows on your bed and a nightstand on each side of your bed.

3. *Make your bedroom your sacred escape.* Your bedroom is a place to relax and rejuvenate. Move the TV, the computer, and any exercise equipment out of the bedroom. Close all doors (including your closet) in your bedroom. Then ask yourself, how can I make my bedroom feel like a sacred oasis? Often, the solution is as simple as adding candles and/or plants, rearranging the space, or removing unwanted distractions.

4. *Your art carries an emotion, so choose wisely.* Everything you display in your house creates a feeling. If you want to experience companionship and joy but you have a painting of a sad woman, alone, sitting by a pond, the energy created by that art isn't aligned with what you want. Surround yourself with art and pictures that bring a smile to your face.

5. *Create a warm "Welcome home!" feeling at the entrance to your home.* What's the first thing that welcomes you when you enter? Is it a pile of shoes on the floor, or something that makes you smile? In my entryway I have framed photos of favorite memories and a sign that says, "We're happy you're here!" It always makes me smile.

6. *Circulate fresh air.* Make sure to open windows to allow fresh air in. In the winter I only do this for a minute, but that burst of fresh air makes all the difference in the air quality and my mood. I like to use an affirmation: "As I open my windows and let in fresh air, I purify my space from worry and stuck energy."

7. *Fix what is broken.* Your space reflects you. If it's broken, fix it or let it go.

8. *Light up your life!* The lighting in your space has a drastic impact on your mood. Do what you can to let natural sunlight in. Follow nature by having the option for soft lighting at nighttime to allow your body to know it's time to wind down. I recommend a light switch dimmer.

9. *Do a space clearing.* Grab a stick of sage, palo santo, or your favorite incense and walk around the house, making sure to target corners. Imagine the smoke purifying your space and releasing stuck energy. I do this once each season throughout my house, making sure to open windows in every room. I find it incredibly cleansing. I can't say for sure that it's the sage, but the house does feel better each time I do it. There is power in rituals and intentions. If nothing else, it's an excuse to open every window in the house, which by itself purifies the space.

Creating Your Sacred Space

As an additional step, if you're feeling inspired to take your external environment to the next level, I recommend creating a sacred space in your home. Think of your sacred space, which can be an unused room or simply a corner of a room, as your own personal space.

There are different ways to do this. Here are a couple of suggestions:

- Select a corner or room that you use specifically as your sacred space. First clear the area of clutter and unhelpful distractions, and then arrange it in ways that inspire in you the feelings you desire.

- Create a ritual to transform a space into your sacred space when you need one. When I was living in a tiny apartment in New York City, I used to roll out my yoga mat in my living room and light a candle once each day when I was ready to tap and meditate. Although the space had multiple purposes throughout the day, each time I did those two things, the space felt sacred to me.

Once your sacred space is ready, make a point of using it to connect to your innermost desires and dreams, to tap, meditate, contemplate, and celebrate. It's where you can go to travel within, whether you have only five minutes or much longer.

Time for the End-of-Chapter Tapping Meditation!

Now that we've looked at how your external environment impacts your getting unstuck, in the next chapter we'll take a look at another big area of life that can support you in creating lasting change—your relationships.

First, though, be sure to check out the Chapter 5 Tapping Meditation.

CHAPTER 5 TAPPING MEDITATION: CLEARING OVERWHELM AROUND CLUTTER

Notice how intensely overwhelmed you feel when you think about clearing clutter. Rate its intensity on a scale of 0 to 10.

Take a deep breath.

Begin tapping on the Karate Chop point.

Karate Chop *(repeat three times)*: Even though I feel completely overwhelmed when I think about clearing clutter, I accept myself and how I feel.

Eyebrow: All this clutter

Side of Eye: How did I let it get so bad?

Under Eye: Just thinking of it makes me feel overwhelmed

Under Nose: It's too much

Under Mouth: I know I should do something about it

Collarbone: But my life already feels overwhelming

Under Arm: I already have so much on my plate

Top of Head: I keep putting it off

Eyebrow: I keep telling myself I'll get to clearing this clutter

Side of Eye: But that day never seems to come

Under Eye: I acknowledge my resistance

Under Nose: Clutter, by nature, is overwhelming

Under Mouth: No wonder this has felt hard

Collarbone: I acknowledge any other feelings that arise

Under Arm: When I think about my clutter

Top of Head: I recognize any disappointment I feel

Eyebrow: When I think about my clutter

Side of Eye: I recognize any worry, fear, or shame that arises

Under Eye: When I think about my clutter

Under Nose: Facing this clutter has felt overwhelming

Under Mouth: Because I've had to face my own judgments

Collarbone: Maybe I can forgive myself?

Under Arm: Maybe I can approach this clutter with a compassionate heart?

Top of Head: Maybe this can be easier than I thought?

Eyebrow: Maybe clearing this clutter can actually feel good?

Side of Eye: I don't have to do it all at once

Under Eye: I can start small

Under Nose: And I savor each success

Under Mouth: I notice how good it feels to take one step

Collarbone: Then the next step feels easier

Under Arm: Maybe this can feel amazing?

Top of Head: Maybe this is the fresh start I've been looking for?

Eyebrow: As I clear clutter in my house

Side of Eye: I clear clutter in my mind

Under Eye: When I celebrate every small step

Under Nose: The next step feels easier

Under Mouth: As I let go of what I don't love

Collarbone: I make room for more love in my life

Under Arm: As I organize my space

Top of Head: My life feels more organized

Eyebrow: I release the need to do it perfectly

Side of Eye: Every small step forward brings me closer to what I desire.

Under Eye: It feels good to let go

Under Nose: It feels good to reclaim my space

Under Mouth: I find the joy in letting go

Collarbone: My environment supports my dreams

Under Arm: I make room in my life for miracles . . .

Top of Head: And I find the joy in every step

Take a deep, cleansing breath. How overwhelmed do you feel now when you think about clearing clutter? Keep tapping until you feel the desired level of peaceful willingness.

Chapter 6

How Healthier Relationships Support Change

As we continue creating change and moving toward flow, it's important to look at how relationships are contributing to the experience of being stuck.

Sometimes we may hesitate to take action and make changes because of how others might react. Also, to get unstuck we have to gain clarity and create movement. That takes energy. Similar to how external clutter stifles flow, relationship stress drains us of the energy we need to create the change we desire.

To gain a clearer understanding of how and why relationship dynamics may be keeping us stuck, we'll look at three different ways that stress typically shows up in relationships. Most of us can relate to all three, not just over a lifetime, but from one relationship to another. For example, we may interact with family differently than we do with friends. Even within a single relationship, we may find ourselves shifting roles over time and as circumstances change. Using this new awareness, we'll then use Tapping to feel calmer and more deeply rooted in our own power within relationships.

Looking at your relationships in this way doesn't mean that you'll never have to make a tough decision or have a hard conversation. It does mean that you'll feel better equipped to do those things from an empowered, positive place that supports you in creating the lasting change you desire.

Afraid of Social Rejection and Isolation? You're Not Alone.

At the heart of much of relationship stress is a core fear that we all share, and that's the fear of rejection. On a rational level, this fear makes no sense. We are, after all, evolved spiritual beings. We know and accept that not every one of the more than seven billion people on the planet will like us. That's just common sense! However, the reason that we suffer from fear of rejection has nothing to do with the rational mind. In fact, we now know that fear of rejection has been hardwired into the primitive brain.

Similar to how the fight-or-flight response dates back to when we lived in the wild with minimal protection, our fear of rejection also stems from early evolution. When we shared our living space with woolly mammoths, saber-toothed tigers, and other fierce creatures, being included in the group was essential for survival. If we were cast aside, we had little chance of fending off or escaping attack.[1]

Although we no longer face those same threats on a daily basis, the primitive brain still thinks that being included by the group is a matter of life or death. Over several thousand years, it's been ingrained in our survival instinct.

I remember first learning about that and having a big *aha!* moment. Finally my fear of being left out, of not being liked and accepted enough, made sense. More importantly, I could approach those moments of fear with more compassion and understanding. Instead of telling myself I was being silly or too sensitive, I used Tapping to begin reprograming my primitive brain to understand that rejection is sometimes a part of life, rather than a matter of death.

Sometimes we also experience rejection in subtler ways. For example, we may feel rejected if someone disagrees with our choices or doesn't actively support changes we're making. When this happens, staying stuck can feel safer than making changes that affect our relationships.

As you begin to look at your role in your relationships, keep in mind that your primitive brain is hardwired to fear social rejection and isolation. Some of the patterns you've developed in relationships may not be ideal, but they *have* enabled you to be accepted. If the idea of changing them is scary, that's because your primitive brain fears that you'll be left out of the group, which it still thinks is life-threatening.

Oftentimes making a change means disappointing others who feel more comfortable with us staying the same. We are born into families where certain roles and expectations are placed upon us without our consent or awareness. The same way that change can feel nerve-wracking to us, change feels unsettling to those around us. The more we understand these dynamics and the roles we play within relationships, the easier it is to navigate through them and make positive changes.

A Bird's-Eye View

Take a moment to think about one relationship in your life that tends to create stress for you. Then ask yourself:

- How do I feel after interacting with this person?
- Do my interactions with him/her fill me up or drain me?

You may also want to ask yourself:

- What topics and conversations recur in this relationship?
- Are these topics and conversations empowering or disempowering; energizing or depleting; inspiring or depressing; or initially exciting, but ultimately draining?

It can also be helpful to tap through the points while asking yourself the questions above.

Next we'll look more specifically at the three roles we tend to play in relationship stress. As you read through them, remember that our goal is to gain clarity, never to blame or shame ourselves. We all play a part in relationship stress, and by being honest and open about it, we can heal old wounds and help to create healthier relationships.

We'll look first at how and why relationship stress happens when we act as the *drama shrinker.*

The Drama Shrinker

The *drama shrinker* shies away from creating drama, often going to great lengths to avoid creating conflict. Toward that end, the drama shrinker may hold onto beliefs like these:

I must always say yes, or else others won't like me.

If I play small enough, I won't disappoint anyone.

Other people's feelings are more important than my own.

If I play small, I'll avoid conflict.

I'm a people pleaser. It's just who I am.

One of my favorite stories about drama shrinking came up during a group workshop one day. At the beginning of the day, I asked if anyone had anything they wanted to share about the previous evening.

Molly raised her hand and said that she had been staying in someone else's home, as she agreed to watch his cat. She explained how annoyed she was to be cat sitting because she's allergic to cats. Her eyes had watered, and she sneezed constantly in the cat's presence. Hoping for relief, she had begun to tap while focusing on her resentment around cat sitting. After a few moments she felt better, and her allergic symptoms had begun to subside. She'd been amazed and was excited about telling the group about her results.

"I'm glad to hear it helped," I responded. "But, Molly, why are you watching a cat when you're allergic to cats?"

Her facial expression turned sheepish, and she quickly looked down at her hands.

"This person I work with told me he had a friend who was desperately looking for someone to watch his cat while he was away. He volunteered me for the job and said I was trustworthy. This cat owner is really picky over who watches his cat." As Molly said this, she smiled at how ridiculous it sounded. "I know, I know, it's crazy, I just felt bad saying no," she said in her defense.

She then explained that this cat required meticulous, painstaking care. The owner had been emphatic and specific about what it required during different parts of each day. Molly had been dutifully fulfilling her obligations, but with each passing day, she felt sicker and sicker.

"So why did you agree to sit for the cat?" I inquired.

"I don't know," Molly began. "The owner was so insistent that he really needed help, and I was the only person who could do it. I just . . . said yes."

Molly knew that saying no would be better for her health and well-being. Nonetheless, she'd placed the cat owner's needs and desires above her own.

Most of us can relate to Molly's desire to please others. We've all said yes when we wanted to say no. We've sacrificed our own well-being because others "needed" us. When we do that, we step into the role of the drama shrinker.

Taking Up Space and Reclaiming Your Voice

Drama shrinkers are so focused on being accepted and liked that they downplay their own needs, desires, and feelings. Many brush off this pattern by labeling themselves as "people pleasers." As a result, they often feel too drained by others to create the change they desire in their own lives.

The challenge of this tendency is that it eventually leads to resentment. The irony is that the drama shrinkers don't actually avoid drama. They just respond to it differently, stuffing down their emotions out of fear that expressing them may lead to rejection or conflict.

Over time these repressed emotions can get stuck in the body and show up as weight gain, headaches, chronic back pain, and more. If we don't learn how to say no to others, the body will say no for us, using symptoms like physical pain, insomnia, and more to get our attention. Eventually our symptoms become so overwhelming that we have no choice but to say no.

Stuck in this pattern of shrinking, drama shrinkers may also ignore intuitive hunches about people whom they sense are unhealthy for them.

Fortunately, Tapping is incredibly effective at giving the body a break, releasing not just the repressed emotion, but also helping to relieve the physical symptoms those emotions may contribute to.

Stepping out of the drama shrinker role begins with creating healthy boundaries. Let's use Tapping to create a sense of safety around speaking up.

Drama Shrinker: Practicing Healthy Boundaries

Saying no can be especially challenging for drama shrinkers, since their aim is to avoid rejection and conflict at all cost.

To begin using Tapping to establish healthy boundaries, start by thinking about a situation where you should or would like to say no. Notice any resistance or anxiety you feel, and write down those feelings.

When I think about saying no, I feel . . .

___ *Like a disappointment*

___ *Guilty*

___ *Nervous*

___ *Like I'm not doing enough*

___ *Like I'm being selfish*

Fill in others here:

_____

_____

_____

Next rate the intensity of your primary (strongest) emotion about saying no on a scale of 0 to 10.

Now let's do some Tapping on releasing those feelings. You can replace words and phrases as needed to make your Tapping as relevant to your experience as possible.

Note: This is a sample Tapping script, with only one negative round and one positive. The complete, expanded script is in the Appendix on page 210.

Take a deep breath.

We'll begin by tapping on the Karate Chop point.

Karate Chop (*repeat three times*): Even though I am so scared of disappointing others that saying no creates anxiety in my body, I accept myself and how I feel.

Sample Negative Round:

Eyebrow: I can't say no

Side of Eye: They need me

Under Eye: And I can't disappoint them

Under Nose: I can't say no

Under Mouth: Just the thought of saying no

Collarbone: Creates anxiety in my body

Under Arm: All this fear

Top of Head: I just want everyone to be happy

Sample Positive Round:

Eyebrow: Whether I say yes or no, I am still a good person

Side of Eye: My happiness is not dependent on their approval

Under Eye: It's safe to say no to others

Under Nose: And yes to myself

Under Mouth: I choose what feels right to me

Collarbone: And I give others the permission to say no

Under Arm: I begin to practice saying no

Top of Head: So that I can say yes to myself

Take a deep breath. When you think of that same situation where you want or need to say no, how do you feel now? Rate the intensity of your primary emotion once again on a scale of 0 to 10. Keep tapping until you can imagine saying no without experiencing any intense negative emotion.

EASING INTO SAYING NO

To help you say no when you need to but worry that you can't, use these great tips from Cheryl Richardson's book *The Art of Extreme Self-Care* on how to respond to requests:

- *Buy yourself time.* Instead of immediately saying yes, gently let them know you'll get back to them. After doing some Tapping on saying no, I asked Molly to pause before answering any and all requests, including ones she was excited about, for at least seven days. When I followed up with her several months later, she recalled how helpful this practice had become. Giving herself time before replying has allowed her to make healthier, more balanced decisions around when to say no and when to say yes. When the cat owner asked her to cat sit a second time, she was able to say no and feel confident about her decision.

- *Do a gut check.* Be really honest with yourself about how you want to respond. What's the best answer—not for the other person or the situation, but *for you?* Ask yourself, *If I wasn't worried about other people's reactions, how would I respond to this request?*

- *Tell the truth directly—with grace and love.* When it's time to say no, make sure to be honest while also being loving and gracious. Express your appreciation and thanks for the invitation or offer you were given, and then be honest about why it doesn't work for you. You don't need to go into extreme detail; just give them a reason why you can't say yes and then move on. If they won't accept your answer, repeat it and gently let them know that you have to go or hang up or whatever is appropriate.

Tapping through Affirmations: Drama Shrinkers

Another great exercise for overcoming drama shrinking is to tap through affirmations, which can help you identify where your resistance lies. If an affirmation doesn't feel entirely true or authentic, explore the emotions and beliefs that are causing that resistance. By tapping on releasing those limiting emotions and beliefs, you can get into closer alignment with your affirmation. Once that happens, your affirmation can inspire positive growth and action, and support you in growing out of the drama shrinker role.

Read through the following affirmations a few times each. Saying them out loud can be especially powerful in helping you to pinpoint the presence or absence of resistance.

As you say or read each one, be aware of any emotional, mental, or even physical resistance (pain, tension, and the like) you experience. That resistance then becomes your Tapping target. For example, if you feel anxious when you read the affirmation "What I feel matters," you could begin tapping on "This anxiety": "This anxiety about valuing myself and my feelings."

To get you started, here are some affirmations for drama shrinkers:

"What I think matters."

"I can say no with grace."

"There are over seven billion people on earth, and not everyone needs to like me or agree with me."

"My time is valuable, and I consciously choose to be around people who lift me up."

You can also write your own Tapping affirmations:

_____

_____

_____

Begin tapping on any resistance you feel, whether it's doubt, fear, shame, or another emotion. When you can say the affirmation without feeling any resistance, you can do some additional tapping rounds while simply speaking the affirmation and letting yourself feel the positive emotions it creates.

The Drama Fixer

Similar to the *drama shrinker*, the *drama fixer* tends to prioritize others' drama over his or her own feelings, needs, and desires. Instead of shrinking, the drama fixer dives headfirst into other people's problems with the intention of resolving them on others' behalf. Since so much of their time and energy is dedicated to others, drama fixers often feel too busy or drained to create the change they need and desire.

Many drama fixers learned to assume this role in childhood, when they felt like they had to be the adult. Sensing others' pain from a young age, they took on the responsibility of keeping the peace and making things better. Consciously or unconsciously, they then carry this burden into adulthood.

Drama fixers can suffer from the belief that others' struggles are their failures. While on a rational level they understand that they can't and shouldn't control others or their lives, they still tend to blame themselves when loved ones falter.

Drama fixers can also get caught in a pattern of feeling alone and unloved, since others are rarely, if ever, willing to help them as much as they help others. Eventually, drama fixers may also start to resent the people whose lives they're trying to fix, since they never get that same level of support and caring in return.

These are some common beliefs that drama fixers hold on to:

I am responsible for everyone's happiness.

If someone I love is hurting, it's my job to fix it.

If I don't over-give, then everything will fall apart.

I know what's best for everyone around me.

Supporting vs. Fixing

Sometimes it's hard to tell the difference between being a supportive, caring friend and acting as a drama fixer.

I realized at one point several years ago that I was acting as a drama fixer with a friend who was struggling with melancholy after a breakup. Her relationship had ended shortly before an important exam, and she didn't do well on the exam as a result. Worried about the impact the exam might have on her future, I continually spoke up and offered her advice, including encouraging her to tap. She didn't want any part of it and soon began avoiding me.

Realizing that something was off, I sat in silence to reflect on the situation. It soon occurred to me that I didn't know what the right course of action for her was. Pretending that I did know wasn't helping either of us. Also, every time I tried to give her advice, I was unintentionally sending her a message that she's incapable of figuring it out herself.

There are, of course, times we may need to step in to care for an aging relative, sick child, or disabled friend or neighbor. There are also contained periods of time when our extra input and effort may be desired and appreciated. Those are just some examples of offering your support and caring when others need it most.

However, if you continually respond to others' pain with repeated attempts to "fix" their problems, as I did with my friend after her breakup, you may be acting as a drama fixer. Here are some beliefs and behaviors that are common to drama fixers:

- Offering detailed advice about what others should and shouldn't do
- Feeling like you know what's best for other people
- Feeling a sense of purpose and fulfillment when others need you

To begin looking at whether you're acting as the drama fixer in any of your relationships, ask yourself the following questions. As always, try to be curious rather than judgmental as you step back and notice these different ways that drama is playing out in your life.

When someone you love is struggling, do you . . .

- Offer them your love and support or try to tell them what they need to do or not do?
- Blame yourself if you're unable to fix others' issues?
- Regularly sacrifice your own needs and desires in order to help others solve their problems?

Next we'll do some Tapping on overcoming drama fixer tendencies.

Drama Fixer: Letting Go and Finding Peace

If you recognize any of these drama fixer patterns, Tapping is a great way to begin giving yourself the love and caring that you're seeking from others when you step into the drama fixer role.

First rate how intensely you feel the need to "fix" others' lives on a scale of 0 to 10.

Note: This is a sample Tapping script, with only one negative round and one positive. The complete, expanded script is in the Appendix on page 213.

Take a deep breath.

We'll start by tapping on the Karate Chop point.

Karate Chop (*repeat three times*): Even though I feel responsible when others are having a difficult time, I accept how I feel, and stay open to a new way of thinking.

Sample Negative Round:

Eyebrow: I care so deeply

Side of Eye: I want this problem to be resolved

Under Eye: I want to jump in and fix this

Under Nose: But as hard as I try

Under Mouth: I feel disappointed

Collarbone: It's hard to see someone I love suffer

Under Arm: I suffer along with them

Top of Head: And experience overwhelming worry

Sample Positive Round:

Eyebrow: I recognize this pattern of feeling responsible

Side of Eye: And I honor my desire to help

Under Eye: I've been trying to control the outcome

Under Nose: And it's only caused me worry and pain

Under Mouth: I'm open to a new way

Collarbone: I'm open to receiving divine help

Under Arm: I can only give what I feel inside

Top of Head: I choose to feel peace

Take a deep breath. Rate the intensity of your need to "fix" others' lives again on a scale of 0 to 10. Keep tapping until you feel more peace with the idea of relieving yourself of the responsibility of fixing others' problems.

Tapping through Affirmations: Drama Fixers

Following are affirmations that you can tap through, first to notice where your resistance lies, and then to step out of the drama fixer role in your relationships.

Read through the following affirmations a few times each, noticing any emotional, mental, or even physical resistance (clenching, tightness, fatigue, and so on) you experience. That resistance becomes your Tapping target.

Here are some affirmations for drama fixers:

"I am not responsible for anyone else's happiness but my own."

"It's my job to love, not to fix."

"I trust in their spiritual journey."

"They will discover what's best for them."

You can also write your own Tapping affirmations:

_____

_____

_____

Begin tapping on any resistance you feel, whether it's fear, anger, doubt, or another emotion. When you can say the affirmations without feeling any resistance, you can do some additional tapping rounds while simply speaking the affirmations and letting yourself feel the positive emotions it creates.

Next we'll look at the third role we may sometimes fall into—the *drama seeker*.

The Drama Seeker

One day I was teaching a seminar, discussing the three main ways that drama shows up in relationships, when Sara raised her hand. A prolific painter, Sara had never shared her work with agents or galleries. Most of her friends had hardly even seen her art! What she had been doing, however, was creating drama in her intimate relationship. That drama, she confessed, was keeping their relationship from getting boring.

In that particular relationship, Sara was acting as the *drama seeker*, creating drama to avoid facing the lack of love and connection she felt with her boyfriend. Drama had also become an all-consuming distraction, giving her an excuse to avoid putting her art out in the world. Her drama-seeking behavior was preventing her from focusing on the career changes that she'd long wanted to create.

I was so impressed by Sara's honesty and courage that I may have thanked her for sharing a few dozen times! We're taught that creating drama is shameful, so we understandably shy away from opportunities to see ourselves as the ones causing it. The one thing I'm fairly sure of is that we all, at some point or another, play an active role in creating drama. And you know what? That's okay! Our goal here is simply to observe without judgment the different roles that we're playing in our relationships. Then we can heal the patterns that support and perpetuate drama.

With that in mind, let's look at some of the most common characteristics of the drama seeker:

- Consciously or unconsciously seeking drama
- Believing that drama is stressful but also exciting
- Enjoying the unpredictability of drama
- Feeling a greater sense of connection through fighting
- Being inclined toward testing love and loyalty through conflict
- Talking about drama at length, focusing on the problem without any real inclination toward solving it
- Being quick to anger, often based on assumptions (e.g., get cut off on highway and assume that person is out to insult/degrade them)
- Bragging about their drama
- Boosting their own value by talking about drama while still feeling like the victim of drama
- Feeling easily bored in the absence of drama

If you recognize any of these traits in yourself, there's no need to label yourself as a drama seeker across the board. Most of us engage in drama-seeking behavior at certain times and with certain people. You may play very different roles in other relationships.

Our Collective Search for Excitement

While we're often quick to judge and dismiss drama seekers as "drama queens," as a culture we also tend to glorify drama. We entertain ourselves by watching dramatic movies. We consume television shows about relationships that feed on drama. We click most often on the day's most dramatic news headlines.

This widespread emphasis on drama has two results. First, we may unconsciously take on the belief that we need drama to make life interesting. Over time we become conditioned to crave the excitement that drama brings. Second, we may develop a high tolerance for drama, which may make us partially numb, or at least unaware of how much of our time and energy is being consumed by drama.

The Pleasure (and Pain) of Drama

Drama is a way of attempting to create love and connection, which is a healthy, natural impulse that we all share. What's unhealthy is trying to meet that need through drama, in part because of the very real physical consequences that drama produces.

The human brain is highly adaptive, which means that it will get used to whatever circumstances we create. Over time, if we continually seek out drama as a way of experiencing the love and connection we crave, we unconsciously train the brain to equate drama with love and connection. The brain then adapts to this reality by releasing endorphins in response to drama. As a result of this flood of endorphins, we experience a natural, temporary "high."

On the flip side, when we don't have drama, we're likely to experience some degree of physical, mental, and emotional trauma. Since we're not getting the drama-fueled endorphin rush we've learned to crave, we feel bored, tired, and depleted. This happens because in a state of trauma, the brain instructs the body to get rid of necessary minerals.

In other words, because we've trained the brain to desire drama (a habit that often starts at a young age, before we could recognize what we were doing), the brain has learned to rely on drama. By that point the brain has essentially become addicted to drama. In its absence the brain uses the body to convince us that we need drama. Before long, often without consciously realizing it, we seek out more drama, if only to regain our energy and feel better. This ongoing thirst for drama is a distraction that robs us of the time and energy we need to create the change we desire.

The Bonding Power of Gossip

One of the most common ways that drama seeking shows up in our lives is through gossiping. Before we look at this habit more closely, it's important to differentiate between healthy venting and gossiping.

As one example, if you hear that a friend got the job (or the date, promotion, or similar) that you wanted, you might call a different mutual friend to discuss the situation and even the jealousy you feel about it. As long as that conversation is focused on processing how you feel, rather than judging it or the successful person, you're engaged in healthy venting. If, however, that conversation devolves into negative judgments about the friend (or the job or whatever it may be), and you find yourselves saying hurtful things that you would never say to that person directly, then you're gossiping.

Let's again be honest about a couple of things. First, we all gossip sometimes. Also, for short periods of time, it *is* entertaining! There's no need to feel shame about that. Most of us learned how to gossip at a young age, and quickly noticed that it creates a fast, although fleeting, sense of connection between people. Gossiping is an easy way to be part of the group, which relieves our primal fear of social isolation.

On rare occasions gossiping can also be harmless. However, when it's a regular habit or a central part of a relationship, gossiping creates unhealthy connection. Instead of building and strengthening relationships, gossiping ultimately chips away at the trust that's essential to deep, lasting connection.

When you focus on your own experience around gossiping, begin by asking yourself these questions:

- Is the example I'm thinking of actual gossiping or just healthy venting?
- If it is gossiping, how does it make me feel?
- If it creates a sense of connection or intimacy, how can I find a healthier way to create that same feeling?

Drama Seeker: Observing Drama

When we're really upset about a situation, even when we're acting as a drama seeker, it can be really hard to step back and notice the role we're playing in drama. By using Tapping to process your feelings, you can feel more empowered within drama. You're then likely to act and react to situations differently.

Let's do some Tapping on that now.

Note: This is a sample Tapping script, with only one negative round and one positive. The complete, expanded script is in the Appendix on page 216.

Begin by taking a deep breath.

We'll start by tapping on the Karate Chop point.

Karate Chop *(repeat three times)*: Even though I feel like drama always finds me, I honor my experience and I am open to a new way.

Sample Negative Round:

Eyebrow: Part of me is tired of this drama

Side of Eye: But I don't know how to end it

Under Eye: If I'm not upset, then it means I won't be heard

Under Nose: If they don't argue with me

Under Mouth: It means they don't care

Collarbone: I've been using drama to test my relationships

Under Arm: Part of me is tired of this drama

Top of Head: Part of me feels powerless to change it

Sample Positive Round:

Eyebrow: I begin to see what I'm truly craving

Side of Eye: I'm craving love

Under Eye: I'm craving connection

Under Nose: I want to feel heard

Under Mouth: And as I begin to give myself my own love

Collarbone: As I begin to connect with myself

Under Arm: As I begin to listen to my inner voice

Top of Head: It's easy to walk away from drama

Take a deep breath. Keep tapping until you feel less attached to the drama and more willing to step away from it without experiencing negative emotions like fear, boredom, and so on.

Tapping through Affirmations: Drama Seekers

Once again, tapping through affirmations is a great way to notice where your resistance lies.

To begin, read through each of the following affirmations a few times each. As you do, be aware of any emotional, mental, or even physical resistance (pain, tension, and the like) you experience. That resistance then becomes your Tapping target.

Some affirmations for drama seekers are:

"I honor my passionate spirit and refocus this energy for good."

"I allow myself to go within before I express how I feel. Peace begins with me."

"I can release the need to fight to be seen. I am loved and valued for who I am."

"Others don't need to agree with me in order for me to experience inner peace."

"What others say is a reflection on them. I choose to not take it personally."

"I remain focused on what matters."

You can also write your own Tapping affirmations:

_____

_____

_____

Begin tapping on any resistance you feel, whether it's doubt, fear, shame, or another emotion. When you can say an affirmation without feeling resistance, you can do some additional tapping rounds while simply speaking the affirmation and letting yourself feel the positive emotions it creates.

Recalibrating to a Newer, Happier "Normal"

Oftentimes it's not until after making positive changes in relationships that we realize how much relationship stress used to affect us. That was the case for Robin, who called in to a teleseminar one day to tell the group how her life had transformed after tapping on her role in relationship stress.

"I have room for myself now!" she exclaimed, her joy resonating clearly in her voice.

Since using Tapping to take a look at relationship drama in her life, Robin had gained clarity on how she was contributing to it. That had led to simple changes in how she was acting and reacting to her closest friends and family. Ever since, the drama had faded away, and she'd felt lighter, freer, and happier. She was making changes in her own life faster than she'd imagined possible, largely because without drama, she could make herself more of a priority.

Now that we've lessened relationship stress and freed up all this energy, in the next chapter we'll look at how to use it to support the most important person in your life—you!

Time for the End-of-Chapter Tapping Meditation!

Instead of a single Tapping Meditation for this chapter, I've included an extended Tapping script for each drama type—*drama shrinker*, *drama fixer*, and *drama seeker*—in the Appendix. Use whichever one resonates most before moving to the next chapter. You can find all three scripts in the Appendix beginning on page 210.

when you practice self-care you hear the wise whispers of your intuition

Chapter 7

Making Room for You

When we're feeling stuck, our knee-jerk reaction is to try to push onward. We resist the opportunity to look *inward* and instead tell ourselves to keep going. This tendency to deprive ourselves of regular self-care is part of the pattern of panic.

Because we're avoiding looking within and skimping on self-care, we may default to self-sabotaging behaviors like overeating, binge-watching TV, endlessly surfing the Internet, and procrastinating on things we care about. Although these behaviors keep us feeling stuck over the long term, in the moments when we choose them, we're doing so to give ourselves the rest we crave.

We tell ourselves that we're fine, that life is crazy, that we'll take better care of ourselves, but not today. Today we'd rather find any easy way to numb out; today self-care feels like another item on our to-do list. Since we're taking action from a frantic and fearful place, we eventually hit a wall. We become exhausted, maybe even sick, and only then can we give ourselves the attention and care we deserve.

This ongoing cycle perpetuates limiting beliefs that encourage us to practice self-care only when it's an absolute necessity, rather than on a regular basis.

Similar to how unsupportive environments and relationships hold us back, this limiting cycle around self-care prevents us from feeling good enough to create the change we desire. Feeling stuck is a call to pay attention to ourselves.

It's an invitation to go within and give ourselves the care we so willingly give others. Only then do we find the answer we are looking for and gain the energy to take steps forward.

In this chapter, we'll take a look at some of the most common myths around self-care and then look at easy, powerful tips for adding more of it to your daily life. Self-care isn't just something you should do; it's an absolute necessity when you are creating lasting change.

The Real Reason Self-Care Matters

Rest is prior to motion and stillness prior to action.

— Taoist philosophy

When we're stuck in the pattern of panic and avoiding self-care, we're also more prone to prioritizing others' happiness over our own. It's ironic, really, because we can't give what we don't feel ourselves. When we don't feel centered, we can't help others feel centered. Similarly, when we don't feel happy, we can't support others' happiness.

We know and trust in the simple truth that we can't give what we don't have. Yet still we fall for the trap of self-sacrifice and do much more for others than we do for ourselves. You've heard it before, but I'll say it again:

In order to create lasting change, and in the process be our best and give our best, we have to care for ourselves first.

That statement is true and real and one I live by, but it's also how we, as a culture, have justified self-care. That became starkly apparent to me one day while interviewing Cheryl Richardson, best-selling author of *The Art of Extreme Self-Care*. What she said has had a profound impact on me, helping me rethink why self-care matters so much:

"The acceptable thing for me to say is, honey, if you take better care of yourself, then that means you'll be a better person to be around. While that's true, what I really want to say as I've gotten older is, honey, if you take better care of yourself, the negative self-talk is going to stop. Honey, if you take better care of yourself, you're going to feel stronger in your body. Honey, if you take better care of yourself, you're going to care more about what you think and less about what other people think. And then you're going to be more powerful in the world. You're going to effect change in your life and in the lives of the people around you."

If self-care has such a profound impact on how we feel about ourselves and how we show up in the world, why does it feel hard to give ourselves the time and attention we need?

Why We Resist Self-Care

Genna was attending one of my weekend workshops when she shared her own challenges around practicing regular self-care.

"If I don't wake up early and take the first hour of the day to myself, I get grumpy, and that lowers my productivity. Even my kids encourage me to stick with it because they see the difference it makes. Still, though, I can't let go of this guilt [that I should be working more]."

Her guilt, she added, usually showed up as her boss's voice, which she heard in her head, telling her to increase her sales numbers. Although she regularly hits her sales goals, every time she does, he demands more. Each time he sets her goals higher, Genna wonders if she should take that first hour of each day to do more work. She then reminds herself that she gets grumpy and becomes less focused and less productive when she skips her "me" hour. "I know this [hour in the morning] is what I need," she added, "but the guilt, oh the guilt!"

Do you guilt yourself out of regularly taking time for self-care? Do you take time for self-care and then feel guilty the whole time?

When we slow down and begin to pay attention to our own thoughts and feelings, the critical voice can initially be louder than the whispers of our intuition. We often need to get through the judgment that says, "You should be doing more!" or "You're being selfish!" before we can get quiet and access our inner wisdom that tells us that self-care is essential to getting unstuck.

This story that we must sacrifice to be worthy didn't start with us. It comes from the generations before us.

When you try to quiet your mind and body, what messages do you hear? Refer back to Chapter 2 to tap on the critical voice.

Saying Yes to Self-Care

When Genna realized that her morning "me" hour was something she had to say yes to, not just for her work and sales numbers, but for herself and her family, she also realized that she had to say no to something else—her guilt.

Saying yes to one thing means saying no to others. The fact is, the nos we have to say in order to have time and energy for self-care may or may not be well received. Genna's boss may always prefer that she work longer and longer hours. However, to truly care for ourselves, we have to learn to be okay with others' mixed reactions to the healthy boundaries we must set. If we wait for everyone's approval, we're forced to say no to self-care, which is what got us stuck in the first place.

Ann, a registered nursing assistant, experienced the tension caused by her saying yes to self-care while taking a scheduled day off from work. While swimming after work the night before (part of her effort to practice more self-care), she missed a call. When she later listened to her voicemail, her stomach dropped. The missed call was a request for her to come in to work on her day off.

Ann felt conflicted. While she could use the money and had always said yes when people needed her, she also felt that she needed time for herself. Instead of immediately returning the call, Ann paused to do some Tapping. She realized that she needed to take her scheduled day off.

Feeling nervous about saying no, she tapped again before calling her office back. She then called and gracefully explained that she wouldn't be able to come in on the day they needed her. The office secretary responded, "Oh, Ann, you're breaking my heart." To her surprise Ann replied, "Sorry I can't help. I'm sure it will work out."

When Ann hung up the phone, she was shocked that she'd stood her ground. Soon, though, doubt began to creep in. She once again began tapping, this time repeating the words "Oh, Ann, you're breaking my heart." She tapped through those words until they no longer triggered her. By the end of her Tapping, Ann felt proud of herself for saying no.

After Ann said no to working that day, a friend invited her on a sunset cruise. Because she'd successfully preserved her day off, Ann was able to say yes to a unique and enjoyable experience.

Rather than shunning her critical voice, which was telling her to feel guilty about saying no, Ann used Tapping to neutralize the emotional impact it was having on her. That's how we set healthy boundaries with others and with our own critical voice. We don't ever want to erase or mute that voice inside us; it's a necessary part of our survival instinct. Our goal instead is to listen to what the critical voice has to say without giving it power over us. We can also learn to do the same with others' negative reactions to our boundaries. Although saying no may feel uncomfortable at first, Tapping allows us to let go of that discomfort. Over time, each no becomes easier.

The Three Myths of Self-Care

The guilt we may feel is often compounded by the myths we hold on to about self-care. While there are many cultural beliefs around what's considered acceptable when it comes to self-care, we'll focus on the three myths that seem to be most limiting and also most pervasive.

Self-Care Myth #1: My value comes from how much I give and how much I sacrifice.

In my first book, *The Tapping Solution for Weight Loss & Body Confidence*, this is how I explained this particular myth:

Countless generations of women have been taught that self-sacrifice makes us better and that self-care and pleasure make us selfish and wrong. These ideas tend to be passed down from one generation to the next in ways that are both conscious and unconscious.

Keep in mind, although that particular book was written for women, this myth isn't necessarily gender-specific. Women and men alike have been taught that the more we sacrifice—the more we put into work, family, home, community, and so on—the more valuable we are. In other words, we've allowed our worth to be defined by what we do and how much we give, rather than who we are.

There's a great episode of *Seinfeld* that underscores the prevalence of this myth. George Costanza, one of the main characters, works in management for the New York Yankees baseball team. During lunch one day with his friends Jerry and Elaine, George hilariously demonstrates how he intentionally looks annoyed at work in order to appear busy. His strategy works so well that he's eventually called into the team owner's office to discuss ways to relieve the stress and pressure he's feeling as a result of all of his "hard work." The assumption is, the angrier and more stressed you are, the harder you're working and the more value you're providing. George used this cultural belief to his full advantage!

This cultural myth that we're more valuable when we give more and do more is also partly why we tend to emphasize how busy we are. Busy-ness is how we measure and boost our value. Our jam-packed schedules and to-do lists can seem like proof that we're needed and wanted, that we're giving and doing enough to be valuable. Of course, giving can also be a healthy impulse, but when it comes from a place of needing to prove our worth and value, it can quickly cause us to get stuck.

On a practical level, by buying into this myth that our value is equal only to how much we give and sacrifice, we stifle our ability to rest, reset, and rejuvenate. We deplete the physical, mental, emotional, and creative resources we need to create change, and then refuse ourselves the opportunity to refill our tanks. Over time we feel so run down that we get even more stuck, and eventually we may also suffer from health issues.

By stepping back and noticing when and how this myth shows up in our thoughts, emotions, and lives, we can prevent it from controlling us.

To begin releasing this belief, refer to the Chapter 7 Extended Tapping: Releasing the Limiting Belief "I can't take a break if I want to succeed" on page 218 of the Appendix.

Self-Care Myth #2: I have to earn self-care.

Even when we're aware of how essential self-care is to getting unstuck and creating positive, lasting change, we often have rules in our head about what needs to happen before we're allowed to take time for ourselves.

One rule we make is "I can take care of myself once everyone else is happy." As Genna's boss demonstrated, however, enough is never actually enough. She was consistently among the top salespeople in her company, yet her boss never stopped pushing her to reach higher and higher numbers.

The reality is others will always need and want more from us. If we make others' happiness our top priority, we give ourselves an ongoing reason not to practice regular self-care. By skimping on self-care, we detach from the whispers of our soul that are among our most powerful allies in getting unstuck. We deprive ourselves of the care that will move our lives forward.

This same way of thinking comes into play around our to-do lists. We promise ourselves self-care once the list is done, only to find the list growing. This way of thinking, whether it's applied to task or to others' happiness, is part of the drama-fixer mentality we discussed in Chapter 6. When we fall into this trap, we limit ourselves and our relationships. We also increase our chances of staying stuck.

To begin releasing this limiting belief, follow the Chapter 7 Extended Tapping: Releasing the Limiting Belief "I have to earn self-care" on page 221 of the Appendix.

Self-Care Myth #3: The more I push, the further I'll go.

In a culture that emphasizes achieving over being, it's easy to get lost in the idea that pushing will get us farther. The reality is, the more we push, the faster we experience burnout.

As we've seen, this emphasis on always pushing is part of the pattern of panic. It's one way that the critical voice can control us. Think about it. Was there a time (or several) when you were self-critical and you tried to push yourself to change or fix something about yourself or your life? Did pushing prove sustainable, or did it work only for a period of time before you couldn't keep it up any longer?

When we try to push ourselves to always do more, we're usually consistent for a contained amount of time. Inevitably, though, we get exhausted and give up because we're so focused on pushing, we forget to balance it out with self-care.

If, however, we make time and space for self-care, we can, when necessary, push ourselves to get things done *without* experiencing burnout.

To begin releasing this belief, refer to the Chapter 7 Extended Tapping: Releasing the Limiting Belief "The more I push, the further I'll go" on page 223 of the Appendix.

Tips for Practicing (and Enjoying!) Self-Care

Now that we've looked at some of the myths that prevent us from practicing self-care, let's look at six tips for how to integrate self-care that rejuvenate us and move us toward lasting change and flow.

1. Remember that self-care is meant to be easy.

Our achievement mentality often spills over into what we define as self-care. To practice self-care, you don't need to do yoga, meditate for an hour, and drink green juice. Self-care is about taking the pressure off of doing and giving more. It's your time for yourself, and you can use it however you wish. It's about pleasure and enjoyment and doing whatever it is that fills you up. The best self-care isn't complicated, costly, or hard to get to. It's easy and accessible, and therefore something you can easily do more often.

2. Take 15 minutes to check in with yourself.

When was the last time you slowed down to ask yourself, *How am I doing?*

Taking 15 minutes to check in with yourself creates space in your day to do some Tapping, meditate, or do whatever else fills you up. It's in these moments of stillness that we connect with our intuition and get answers.

Although these quiet moments provide huge value, we sometimes resist the invitation to get still because our intuition or body might tell us things we don't feel ready to hear. However, if we don't listen to these messages, we can't get unstuck and find our flow. By allowing ourselves to hear these messages, we can seek relief.

3. Unplug. Be Bored.

*Almost everything will work again if you unplug it for a
few minutes, including you.*

— Anne Lamott

While having dinner out with my husband one night, I noticed myself grabbing my phone the moment he got up to go to the restroom. I instantly checked my social media feeds, as well as e-mail. With our tablets and smartphones and portable, accessible gadgets, it's become incredibly easy to distract ourselves. However, by relying so heavily on social media and technology, we also detach from the present moment. We rob ourselves of the chance to enjoy *being*.

Since that night out, I do my best not to pick up my phone. Instead I look around, take in the aroma of fresh food, enjoy the ambiance, or just let myself daydream.

Would your mood and mind-set change with less exposure to social media and online communication? One study of 1,787 adults between 19 and 32 years old found that social media exposure significantly increased depression.[1]

I often hear people bemoan that they don't have time for themselves. If you've ever said that, put your phone away. You may be surprised how easy it is to find a moment to yourself, even if it's just to look out the window.

4. Wander.

Webster defines wandering as moving about without a fixed course, aim, or goal.

When was the last time you did something that didn't have a final destination or outcome? How often do you let yourself wander?

Last year I took watercolor painting class. I took it for no reason, and quickly discovered that I'm terrible at it. I really enjoyed the whole experience, though! It was creative exploration that had no particular purpose. I don't have any big accomplishments to show from the class, but trying my hand at watercolor felt *really* good.

One easy way to wander is to take a walk without any agenda, not for exercise or for adding steps, but to breathe fresh air. Walk without a goal or destination in mind, and notice how you feel and what you discover.

5. Make Fun a Priority.

Fun for its own sake nearly always counts as self-care.

Sometimes fun means going to the party. Sometimes it means saying no so you can watch a movie at home.

Fun comes in many flavors. It can be gardening, cooking, or reading. It can be sledding down a hill after a snowstorm, dancing in your living room, or appreciating the flowers in springtime.

Try making fun a higher priority and see how it affects you.

6. Stop and smell the roses, or your coffee.

One day while a Brazilian cousin was visiting me, we had lunch and afterward walked into a coffee shop. I assumed we'd get coffee and then get in the car to head home. As we walked to the door, however, she grabbed a seat. I smiled, remembering that to her getting coffee means sitting down and enjoying it.

In Brazil, as well as Argentina, Paris, and many other parts of the world, you can't order coffee to go unless you're at Starbucks. That's because coffee is more than a drink. It's an experience, a chance to slow down and savor.

That day I sat down with my coffee and my cousin; we chatted and connected. It was relaxing, and also a valuable reminder to slow down and savor. When we find the delight in small things, we feel lighter and more joyful.

None of these simple self-care tips require money. Nor do they need lots of time, energy, or effort. However, the calm and peace they produce allows us to find clarity more easily. By making self-care a higher priority, we're better able to know what we need and what we want. At that point we can set powerful intentions for creating lasting change. That's what we'll do in the next chapter.

Time for the End-of-Chapter Tapping Meditation!

Before moving on, make sure to use the Chapter 7 Tapping Meditation.

CHAPTER 7 TAPPING MEDITATION:
RELEASING SELF-CARE GUILT

When you think about taking time to practice regular self-care, how guilty do you feel? Rate the intensity of your guilt on a scale of 0 to 10.

Take a deep breath.

Begin tapping on the Karate Chop point.

Karate Chop *(repeat three times)*: Even though I feel guilty every time I take care of myself, I honor how I feel and I am open to a new way.

Eyebrow: I know I should take more time for myself

Side of Eye: But it feels impossible

Under Eye: I have so much going on

Under Nose: So much I should be doing

Under Mouth: So many people depend on me

Collarbone: And there's so much I still need to get to

Under Arm: Taking time for myself feels wrong . . .

Top of Head: When I have so much I should be doing

Eyebrow: Part of me wants to take this time

Side of Eye: Another part of me feels guilty

Under Eye: Where did I pick up this belief?

Under Nose: This belief that self-care is wrong

Under Mouth: When did I learn that I have to sacrifice . . .

Collarbone: And put others' needs above my own?

Under Arm: I was taught that that was how the world works

Top of Head: I was taught that in order to be a good person

Eyebrow: I have to put others' needs above my own

Side of Eye: I always come last

Under Eye: And I'm so tired of it

Under Nose: But I can't see any other way

Under Mouth: Because things will fall apart

Collarbone: If I'm not trying to control everything

Under Arm: Is this really true?

Top of Head: I recognize this as a belief

Eyebrow: It's been passed down for generations

Side of Eye: It's what society is telling me

Under Eye: But the price is too high

Under Nose: I recognize how tired I am

Under Mouth: I recognize I need time for myself

Collarbone: I thought it was a sign of weakness

Under Arm: But I now realize it's a sign of courage and strength

Top of Head: By saying no to others, I say yes to myself

Eyebrow: I acknowledge any remaining guilt

Side of Eye: It's a pattern that's been passed down to me

Under Eye: And I choose to release it

Under Nose: I release it for myself and future generations

Under Mouth: Self-care is food for the soul

Collarbone: As I nurture myself

Under Arm: I begin to bloom in unexpected ways

Top of Head: And I inspire others to do the same

Eyebrow: Anytime I hear the whisper of guilt

Side of Eye: I let it go

Under Eye: That guilt never belonged to me

Under Nose: I can pave a new way for myself

Under Mouth: It is safe to take care of myself

Collarbone: It is safe to let go and relax

Under Arm: I begin to hear the whispers of my intuition

Top of Head: It feels so good to feel good

Take a deep breath. Again notice the intensity of your guilt around practicing more regular self-care. Keep tapping until you experience the desired release.

your job
is to let your
mind and Body
know it's safe
to CHANge

Chapter 8

Dump the Pressure and Fall in Love with Life

It was the 2016 Golden Globe Awards. Comedic actor Jim Carrey strolled on stage, grinning his vaguely devious signature grin. As the audience's applause roared, he began his awards presentation with this:

"Thank you. I am two-time Golden Globe–winner Jim Carrey. You know, when I go to sleep at night, I'm not just a guy going to sleep. I'm two-time Golden Globe winner Jim Carrey going to get some well-needed shut-eye.

"And when I dream, I don't just dream any old dream. No, sir. I dream about being three-time Golden Globe–winning actor Jim Carrey. Because then I would be enough. It would finally be true, and I could stop this terrible search for what I know ultimately won't fulfill me."

I love that both because it makes me laugh and because it paints such an accurate picture of how we relate to goals. We focus on what we don't yet have, haven't yet done, and whom we don't yet know, and set goals to "fix" the lack we feel. In that process we put our critical voice in charge, so even when we do achieve our goals, we quickly find new ones to measure ourselves against.

We cycle through this process repeatedly, not because we want to torture ourselves, but because we've been taught to navigate the process backward.

In this chapter we'll first look at traditional goal setting and how it can keep us stuck. Then we'll explore a more authentic and powerful approach to moving our lives forward.

When Goals Backfire

People crave success because they hope it will deliver salvation from the ego's self-attack. They hope that being able to say "I've made it" will silence their inner taunts.

— Robert Holden

Goals and I have been in a long-term and often turbulent relationship. I began setting goals in high school, soon after picking up that first self-help book. Research supports that goal setting can make you as much as two times more likely to meet a goal. That being said, in my own life and with clients, I've also experienced how goals can backfire. It's important to recognize the downside of goal setting so we can gain clarity around our desires and pursue them in a more empowered way.

Here are three big ways goal setting affects how we think and feel—about ourselves, our lives, and the future:

1. *Goals can take us from dread to disappointment.* If we succeed in overcoming our dread around setting goals in the first place, we quickly sink into disappointment after creating them. That's often because of our past experience with goals—we set them, perhaps repeatedly, and reached them . . . almost never. I experienced this years ago around weight loss. I'd resolve to start a diet, sure that deprivation and self-restriction were necessary. Before long, I'd feel disappointed by my lack of results and frustrated by the lack of pleasure in my daily life. Eventually, I'd resort to binge eating, and the cycle would begin all over again.

2. *Goals can foster a sense of lack.* We look at our goals and quickly notice what we don't have, what we haven't done, whom we don't know. Instead of motivating us, goals root us in that sense of lack. From that

place, we're less likely to make empowering decisions. We're also less likely to take positive action toward realizing them, which puts us back in the cycle of setting goals and achieving them . . . rarely, if ever.

3. *Goals can become a green light for the critical voice.* As Jim Carrey so humorously illustrated, our goals become a reason for the critical voice to take over, turning goals into a list of what needs to happen before we can feel happy and good enough. From there we quickly fall into the pattern of panic and miss out on the joy—and opportunities—available to us in the present.

Goals and Tunnel Vision

As time passes, goals can become even more limiting. That's partly because of how we feel when we first create them—small and stuck. That mind-set is especially challenging because none of us are our most powerful, visionary selves when we're feeling small and stuck. None of us are imaginative or resourceful when we're focused on all that we and our lives are *not*.

While goals may initially *seem* visionary and inspiring, once we grow and evolve into more confident, empowered versions of ourselves, those same goals may prove limiting. That's because goals reflect the limited vantage point we had when we created them. They reflect what we knew (and didn't yet know) when we felt small and stuck.

After beginning the goal-setting process feeling small and stuck, we're likely to give the critical voice even more power to berate and belittle us when we encounter obstacles. We then get discouraged and decide that our biggest, most important goals are "unrealistic." Rather than quieting that critical voice, we may shrink our goals, choosing smaller ones that are less fulfilling, and also more likely to get us stuck . . . again. Compared to our goals, we feel smaller and smaller as time goes on.

These are some of the ways that goal setting can become a self-perpetuating cycle of lack. Ultimately, the cycle fails to deliver the desired results because the lack we feel at the outset of the process attracts more lack, rather than whatever abundance—love, security, health, and so on—we're seeking.

What Do You Really Desire?

Although goal setting may not always deliver the results we hope for, looking at goals can help us to notice something important—what we really desire.

Sometimes we get attached to an outcome, or goal, without noticing that what we really want is to *feel* a certain way. On a conscious level, we know that outcomes don't automatically deliver inner peace, fulfillment, and other desired emotions. Still, though, we sometimes get attached to specific outcomes because we assume that achieving a certain goal will deliver whatever emotions we want to feel.

The true power of manifesting comes from attaching to the emotions we want to feel while detaching from how we think we need to reach that goal or exactly what it needs to look like. Mike Dooley, author of *Notes from the Universe*, explains the process this way:

> *It's common that when we have a dream, we spend our time worrying about HOW we can make it a reality, when the truth is that letting go of those "hows" is the only real way to move closer in the direction of our dreams . . .*
>
> *If you insist on your own very limited notions, not only will you shut out the other possibilities known by the Universe, but you will likely put unnecessary pressure on your talents, forcing them to be the bringer of your gifts . . .*[1]

In other words, mind-set and emotions are magnetic. When we feel lack, we attract more lack. When we feel creative, we attract creativity. When we feel abundant and loving, we attract abundance and love.

You might assume that I'm telling you to ditch goal setting, but I actually don't believe in scrapping the practice altogether. Have you ever moved a plant to a new a spot in your house, or even just turned it around, and noticed that it begins growing in a new direction? That plant is seeking sunshine. To get what it needs, it begins growing in a new way.

We too need a direction to grow in. We need something that pulls us forward. We need some reason to evolve and expand.

So how do we get "there"—back into our flow, creating lasting change that supports us in growing toward our best life?

Uncovering Resistance

The first step in finding that new direction is looking at how we may be subconsciously resisting our desires.

I was at a Hay House conference luncheon years ago when a writer, Lisa, shared a story with me. Her friend had been having a really hard time. When Lisa asked her friend why things weren't working, her friend mentioned how frustrated she felt about her business. It seemed to have promise, but it had been struggling. She couldn't pinpoint what was wrong, but it wasn't taking off the way she'd hoped.

Lisa tapped with her friend on her frustration about how stuck she felt around her business. At one point during their Tapping, Lisa said, "I want to make more money, but I feel like making money isn't spiritual." Her friend teared up as soon as she heard those words. They paused briefly, knowing that they'd just identified the resistance. Then they did several more rounds of Tapping on Lisa's friend's limiting belief around making money.

Months later, Lisa and her friend met up again. To their shared delight, her friend's business had taken off. Lisa asked what had made the difference. Her friend paused and said she thought it was the Tapping they'd done that day on her belief around making money not being spiritual. Lisa had even forgotten about the experience and was shocked that it had had such a powerful impact!

Years ago I also realized that I was subconsciously resisting my desire to be in a loving relationship. Although I'd been dreaming about meeting "the one," I was also carrying a belief that I'd have to shrink in order to be in a relationship. That belief had been impacting my experience around flirting, dating, and how I felt in my own skin. I would go on dates and not mention my work. I would play down my success; and every time I made more money, I had this little voice telling me, "The more you make, the harder it will be to find a man who isn't intimidated." If you asked me about these beliefs, I would claim they weren't true. My logical mind knew that, but the nagging limiting belief was there, and I finally needed to admit it to myself.

I was only seeing two options: I could play small and be in a relationship, or be single but successful and free to shine my light in the world. I recognized this as a limiting belief and determined that I was ready to find a relationship that made me feel free. Every time I met someone who was intimidated by my passion, it didn't mean I needed to shrink; it simply meant the person wasn't right for me.

As I said in my wedding vows years later, "Falling in love with you didn't feel like falling; it felt like flying. I never knew love could make me feel so free." When I got clear on my resistance and fear around love and cleared them, magic happened and I met my husband.

The inner transformation that happens when we use Tapping to release limiting beliefs and other forms of resistance affects how we react and act in the world, how we interact and communicate. Because we feel different, we attract new people and new opportunities.

WHEN YOUR BODY REACTS FIRST

If just saying something elicits an immediate or uncontrollable physical response, like tearing up, gasping, or something similar, you know you've gotten to a core limiting belief. Those physical reactions to triggers are signs that you've gotten clarity on what's really holding you back.

For these outer transformations to happen, we first have to get clear on which beliefs we're unconsciously resisting, so we can then tap on releasing them. Here are some common limiting beliefs that cause us to subconsciously resist our desires:

"If I make more money, I'll be less spiritual."

"If I lose weight, I'll get unwanted attention."

"If I find a romantic relationship, I'll risk getting hurt again."

"If I improve my health, people will expect more from me."

"If get a promotion or a better job, people will be jealous."

"If I decide to pursue a desire, I might find out I'm not good enough."

"If I realize my dreams, my friends or family won't like me or approve."

Do any of these beliefs ring true? If you notice another limiting belief around realizing your goals and desires that feels more relevant, write it down here:

It can be helpful to answer the question, *What's the downside of realizing this goal or desire?*

_____

Now we'll use Tapping in a couple of different ways to release this belief.

Clearing Resistance: Limiting Beliefs

Once you're clear on which limiting belief around achieving your goals and desires feels most relevant right now, rate how true that belief feels on a scale of 0 to 10. Then begin tapping through it and see what you discover, noticing what emotions you feel when you focus on this belief. Once you know that, you can tap on releasing the emotions. As you peel away the layers, you'll find the original belief starts to feel less true.

In the Appendix, on page 225, I share a tapping meditation to clear the limiting belief "Making money isn't spiritual." This tapping meditation is also helpful if you have the belief that making a lot of money makes you a bad person. Remember, you may logically know something isn't true, but if part of you believes it, it impacts your actions.

Clearing Resistance: Noticing Judgments

Another way to discover your blocks is to notice how you may be judging others who have realized similar desires. If you're looking on social media and you see a photo of someone who is in great shape and think, *They must be so self-centered*, you are telling your unconscious mind it's not safe to reach your fitness goals or people will judge you.

When you pass judgment on someone else, you are teaching your subconscious mind that it's not safe for you to have what that person has because you may be judged in the same way.

The good news is when we catch ourselves passing judgment, we can shed a light on unconscious limiting beliefs that we have been reinforcing through our own judgments.

For example, if you think, *He's so rich. He must be greedy* . . .

What your subconscious hears is, "It's not safe for me to make more money because people will think less of me."

If you make this judgment: "Life must be so easy for them because they [have money, are in shape, have a great relationship, and so on]" . . .

What your subconscious hears is, "If life is easy, then it means I'm less valuable and others will feel jealous. It's not safe for me to reach these goals. It's not safe for me to make life easy."

Ask yourself questions like these:

How do I judge others who make a lot of money?

How do I judge others who have found love?

How do I judge others who have the career I aspire to?

How do I judge others based on their appearance?

If you find yourself thinking or saying negative things, notice that. That resistance is keeping you stuck by telling your brain that realizing your desires is unsafe.

Use what you discover as your Tapping targets. So for instance, if you want to start your own business but tend to assume that successful business owners work 24/7, you can begin by tapping on, "Even though I have this belief that being a successful business owner requires me to become a workaholic, I acknowledge this belief and I am open to a new way of thinking."

Your goal is to clear the emotional charge behind your judgments so that you can celebrate others' success and accomplishments. That tells your brain that it's safe for you, too, to realize your own authentic success.

Once the negative charge is less intense or absent from your judgments of others, do some Tapping on the positive possibilities that emerge, such as "Successful business owners can live multifaceted, interesting lives." Keep tapping on positive statements as often as necessary and until they feel true.

A New Kind of Clarity

A few years ago on my birthday, instead of putting so much attention on the external outcomes I thought I wanted, I set my sights on how I wanted to feel. This list resulted from that process:

I easily begin to care less about what other people think so that I more clearly hear the messages from my own heart.

I easily release old and outdated fears around romantic love so that my heart is open to receive my life partner in a way that feels peaceful and liberating.

I easily feel empowered, in control, and competent around money so that I make wise financial decisions that benefit me for years to come.

I easily find myself communicating a powerful and healing message to the world in a way that feels safe, congruent, and fun.

I easily make decisions that benefit my highest good by knowing I am smart enough and I can trust my instincts.

I easily release the need for perfection, trusting that what I create in the moment is divine and enough.

I easily experience harmony, love, and joy with my family and friends while easily releasing any energetic connections to people who don't serve my greater good.

For at least a year afterward, I read through this list each morning. It became my guide, like a warm, loving hand leading me forward. It wasn't a to-do list or a reminder of everything I wasn't, didn't, hadn't. This list was my vision for my best life. Unlike a list of goals, it didn't include specific outcomes. It was a list of how I wanted to *feel.*

More than any list of goals I'd ever had, this list inspired me. It made me *want* to take action. It helped me to feel more joy and purpose in my everyday life. It also gave me plenty of room to grow and evolve.

ARE YOU REALLY OKAY WITH MAKING LIFE EASY?

We've discussed that most of us have been taught to value struggle. We're told that the more we fight for something, the more deserving we are. When we define our self-worth in different terms that are detached from what and how much we accomplish and sacrifice, we can become more accepting of the idea that life can feel good, that realizing our desires can feel easy. That mind-set supports us in creating lasting change without attracting difficult situations that force us to prove our worth through struggle, strife, and sacrifice.

How Do *You* Want to Feel?

Instead of focusing on goals, ask yourself, *How do I want to feel?* Let's begin exploring that now.

Think about one goal you have or have had, and ask, *How do I think achieving this goal will make me feel?*

Select two or three emotions that you most yearn to feel in this area of your life.

Worthy	Playful
Creative	Grateful
Loved	Excited
Loving	Energetic
Safe	Vibrant
Fulfilled	Adventurous
Inspired	Enthusiastic
Free / Liberated	Proud
Open	Confident
Productive	Curious
Powerful	Appreciated
Blissful	Nurtured
Optimistic	Respected
Passionate	Elated
Knowledgeable	Relaxed

If other emotions come to mind, write them down, making sure you have no more than three desired emotions:

———————————————————   ———————————————————

———

———

Getting clear on the emotions you desire is a great start, but even then, we still may experience subconscious resistance toward those desires. Let's look at releasing that next.

Noticing (and Celebrating!) Your Resistance

Resistance can arise in many different forms, and as we've already seen, it often leads us toward clutter, procrastination, and other self-sabotaging behavior.

I've worked with clients who realized that they wanted to feel relaxed and safe with money, but then resisted releasing money anxiety. On a deeper level, they believed that money anxiety was helping them make better decisions. Once they let go of the limiting belief that they needed money anxiety, they were able to make empowering, clear-headed financial decisions that were far more beneficial.

In the Appendix, on page 228, you'll find a tapping meditation to help you clear financial stress so that you feel grounded and powerful to make better financial decisions.

How are you resisting the emotions you desire to feel?

First take a deep, cleansing breath, and read through your list of desired emotions. Select one emotion that feels especially desirable and focus on it.

Now be honest with yourself. Does it even seem possible to feel this emotion on an ongoing basis? Does it feel safe to feel this way?

How is your resistance showing up? Here are some common ways resistance appears:

- Boredom
- Impatience
- Resentment
- Worry
- Fear
- Being easily distracted
- Procrastination
- Clutter (mental, emotional, physical)
- Other (add what you discover here): _____

In order for this process to be as powerful as possible, you need to let yourself notice the different ways resistance is showing up. The more you can be present in those limitations while tapping, the easier it is to release them.

Remember, too, to take a moment to celebrate your newfound clarity! *Aha!* moments give you the power to break out of old limiting beliefs and outdated patterns that haven't served you. I'd even go so far as to say that once you can see your resistance, you're at least halfway there.

Take a deep breath and let yourself feel your resistance to your desired emotions now. Notice also how your resistance shows up in your physical body. If, for instance, you focus on your desire to feel loved and then feel tightness in your shoulders, be aware of that. Scan your body as you let yourself feel the resistance that has been keeping you stuck.

Take more deep breaths and notice what else your resistance brings up. Do you feel other negative emotions you didn't realize you were holding on to? Do old memories come to mind? Certain people or situations?

After taking note of the different ways your resistance is showing up, rate the intensity of your resistance on a scale of 0 to 10.

Take a deep breath.

Begin tapping on your Karate Chop point.

Karate Chop *(repeat three times)*: Even though I feel all this resistance, it's in my body, my mind, my emotions, I honor how I feel and I accept myself.

Eyebrow: All this resistance

Side of Eye: I feel it in my body

Under Eye: It's in my mind

Under Nose: And the negative emotions I feel

Under Mouth: So much resistance around my desire to feel <desired emotion>

Collarbone: It's safe to feel it now

Under Arm: I can let it all come out now

Top of Head: It's safe to feel the full force of my resistance

Keep tapping through the points as you focus on the specific ways your resistance is showing up—"this pain in my back," "this overwhelming fear," "this belief that I can't be spiritual and feel abundant at the same time."

Continue tapping through the points as you give your resistance a voice.

Eyebrow . . . Side of Eye . . . Under Eye . . . Under Nose . . . Under Mouth . . . Collarbone . . . Under Arm . . . Top of Head . . .

Eyebrow . . . Side of Eye . . . Under Eye . . . Under Nose . . . Under Mouth . . . Collarbone . . . Under Arm . . . Top of Head . . .

Eyebrow . . . Side of Eye . . . Under Eye . . . Under Nose . . . Under Mouth . . . Collarbone . . . Under Arm . . . Top of Head . . .

When you feel ready, take a deep breath. Again rate the intensity of your resistance on a scale of 0 to 10. Continue tapping on releasing your resistance as long as you like.

Note: Fully releasing resistance can be an ongoing process, so be patient with yourself and tap whenever you notice it resurfacing.

Each time you tap through more resistance, take a moment to celebrate yourself. It takes a lot of courage and commitment to see, feel, and release these blocks. Each step forward is a new reason to feel more joy.

Optional Tapping Exercise: Still Unsure about How You're Resisting Your Desires?

If you're not immediately aware of how your resistance is playing out, stay open. After all, if you didn't have resistance, you wouldn't be stuck!

In addition to allowing you to let go of your resistance, Tapping is a powerful way to gain clarity. When we release the frustration and pressure around gaining clarity, we are more open to hearing our intuition.

Begin tapping on your Karate Chop point.

Karate Chop *(repeat three times)*: Even though I'm frustrated because I'm not sure what's holding me back, I give myself permission to relax and trust the answers will come.

Sample Negative Round:

Eyebrow: This resistance

Side of Eye: I'm not seeing it yet

Under Eye: It's frustrating

Under Nose: Because I want to figure this out

Under Mouth: This resistance

Collarbone: This frustration

Under Arm: I feel this pressure to find the answers

Top of Head: That's okay

Sample Positive Round:

Eyebrow: I allow my mind to wander

Side of Eye: I don't need all the answers now

Under Eye: As I release the pressure

Under Nose: I can enjoy my curiosity

Under Mouth: What might my resistance be?

Collarbone: What comes to mind?

Under Arm: I give myself time and space

Top of Head: To receive the clarity I desire

Take a deep breath and make notes about any *aha!* moments you had. Give yourself permission to relax and stay open to answers.

Creating Your Intentions

Next let's create a list of intentions around how you want to feel.

You may have noticed in my own intentions list I used the word *easily* in each. That's because I think it's important to embrace ease whenever we can.

Look back at your list of desired emotions. You'll use these to create your intentions by filling in the blanks:

I easily feel _____ and create movement to support that in my life.

I easily feel _____ and notice ways to move my life toward that.

I easily feel _____ and create positive momentum to realize that in my life.

Read through your intentions and notice how you feel. If you experience any resistance, tap on it. If you feel positive reading them, tap on those good feelings to amplify them.

I recommend tapping through these intentions (and others you may want to add later) on a daily basis, or as often as you can. Try to spend 5 or 10 minutes per day tapping on them. Notice resistance as it arises and tap through it. As you release new layers of conscious and subconscious resistance, observe how your intentions feel and how they begin to manifest in your life over time.

LETTING GO OF NEEDING TO MAP OUT "THE HOWS"

When we're accustomed to feeling like we need to map out how we'll manifest our desires, we can easily fall back into the habit of trying to predetermine what Mike Dooley calls "the cursed hows."

If you notice yourself trying to mentally map out how you'll manifest your desires from start to finish, you most likely have a feeling of overwhelm and fear because we can never know all of the answers. It's important to pause and do some Tapping on it. Refer back to the section in Chapter 4, "I need all the answers before I can move forward."

Integrity-Checking Your Vision

To be a powerful part of your life, the sum of your intentions, which we'll call your vision, has to nourish you and encourage you to grow, just like the plant that has to grow in a new direction in order to find the sun.

Your vision should fill you up. It should provide a direction for you to flow toward *with* your joy intact.

If, at any point, your vision starts to feel limiting, stop and notice that feeling. Tap through the points, while asking yourself questions like these:

Is this vision what I want or something I'm pursuing to please others?

Does this vision still inspire my joy?

Does this vision still feel nourishing, or has it become depleting?

Is this vision rooted in my passion and my purpose, or in what others want or expect from me?

Keep tapping until you achieve more clarity.

There may be times when you're simply overtired and in need of extra self-care. There may be times when your vision has become too pointed toward a single outcome. Make any necessary adjustments and tap as often as you need to rediscover your flow while also pursuing your vision.

In the next chapter we'll dive deeper into your vision using a key practice to continue flowing forward—by understanding procrastination. You'll feel huge relief once you realize what procrastination really is.

Time for the End-of-Chapter Tapping Meditation!

First make sure to use the Chapter 8 Tapping Meditation to continue stepping toward your desires, feeling a little more of what you want to feel each and every day.

CHAPTER 8 TAPPING MEDITATION: CLEARING RESISTANCE

When you think about realizing your vision, how intensely do you experience resistance? Rate its intensity on a scale of 0 to 10.

Take a deep breath.

Begin tapping on the Karate Chop point.

Karate Chop *(repeat three times)*: Even though part of me wants this and part of me doesn't, I accept all these parts of me, and I'm open to making this easy.

Eyebrow: Part of me really wants to pursue this vision

Side of Eye: Part of me is really ready to make this change

Under Eye: But another part of me is scared

Under Nose: I acknowledge my own resistance

Under Mouth: Something about realizing this desire . . .

Collarbone: Doesn't feel safe

Under Arm: I become curious as I recognize my resistance

Top of Head: What is the downside of getting what I want?

Eyebrow: Part of me wants this

Side of Eye: And another part of me is scared that . . .

Under Eye: [name your fear]

Under Nose: I recognize all these parts of me

Under Mouth: Part of me wants to make progress

Collarbone: And another part of me feels stuck in fear

Under Arm: I accept and honor all parts of me

Top of Head: It's safe to recognize my resistance

As you continue to tap, become more specific by repeating your unique "downside." What is the downside of getting what you want? Will you have to be more visible? Will you have to risk failing? Will you have to work more or do things you don't love? What is your resistance? That's your downside; give it a voice as you tap through the points.

Eyebrow: [My downside]

Side of Eye: [My downside]

Under Eye: [My downside]

Under Nose: [My downside]

Under Mouth: [My downside]

Collarbone: [My downside]

Under Arm: [My downside]

Top of Head: [My downside]

Eyebrow: As I acknowledge my fear

Side of Eye: I allow my body to relax

Under Eye: As I acknowledge this fear

Under Nose: I begin to question it

Under Mouth: Is this really true?

Collarbone: This belief I've been holding on to

Under Arm: Maybe I can feel good now

Top of Head: In my mind, body, and spirit

Eyebrow: Even good change can feel scary

Side of Eye: I allow myself to ease into it

Under Eye: And move at my own pace

Under Nose: I begin to release my fear

Under Mouth: I remember that I am in control

Collarbone: I embrace success on my own terms

Under Arm: It is safe for me to succeed

Top of Head: It is safe for me to shine

Eyebrow: My resistance was just trying to protect me

Side of Eye: But I am safe

Under Eye: I am powerful

Under Nose: I am ready

Under Mouth: I am in control

Collarbone: I move at my own pace

Under Arm: I embrace success on my terms

Top of Head: It feels better than I imagined

Take a deep, relaxing breath. Check in again on the intensity of your resistance. Keep tapping until you feel the desired release.

Chapter 9

Getting past Procrastination

When you were born, the doctor didn't place you in your mother's arms and say "Congratulations, it's a . . . procrastinator!"

Procrastinating is something we do, not who we are, yet we often find ourselves saying, "I *am* a procrastinator." I remember years ago doing exactly that. I'd complain that I was so good at starting things, but rarely at finishing them. I'd joke that I had a gift for finding 10 things to do when I really needed to focus on a single task.

Procrastination always felt like *the* problem I needed to solve. It was *the* reason I couldn't make positive changes stick. That belief does seem to make sense. After all, if we're stuck in procrastination, we can't take the action that's necessary to create lasting change. However, as I began to look more deeply at procrastination, I realized that procrastination is not what prevents us from creating lasting change. Procrastination is simply a symptom of deeper challenges we're trying to avoid, and it's those deeper issues that we ultimately have to address in order to create lasting change.

Procrastination can show up in different ways, from putting off taking action on a dream to delaying the small things that, like clutter, begin to build up and weigh on you. By addressing the underlying issues that lead us to procrastinate, we can begin to create more ease around moving forward.

Pssst, Your Procrastination Is Trying to Tell You Something

It often seems easier to blame ourselves for *being* procrastinators than to look at the deeper issues that drive us to procrastinate. However, by overlooking the underlying causes of procrastination, we rob ourselves of the opportunity to notice why we're putting off the small tasks and big dreams we *know* are important. When we avoid those deeper truths, we stay stuck in procrastination.

Procrastination may be one or more of the following:

- Procrastination can be a symptom of fear.
- Procrastination can be our intuition telling us now is not the time.
- Procrastination can be our way to seek comfort when something feels difficult.
- Procrastination can be a way to give ourselves a break when we don't have healthy self-care routines in place.

Instead of focusing on trying to rid ourselves of procrastination, we need to get quiet and hear the wisdom behind it. We'll begin by looking at one common fear that leads us toward procrastination—the fear of failure.

The Fear of Failure

When we fear failure, we may default to procrastination as a way of protecting ourselves from feeling that pain again. That, once again, is the primitive brain actively trying to safeguard us from possible future suffering, which it defines as a form of danger.

With Tapping we can address fears around failing and create a more constructive relationship with failure, which is really just the disappointment we feel when our hopes and expectations aren't met. Here are the three elements of the fear of failure that we can focus on in order to clear it:

1. *How you relate to your past failures.* Were you embarrassed, ridiculed, or shamed for trying and failing? Often it's the little events that can stay with us unnoticed. Take some time to process and release those emotions.

2. *How you treat yourself when you make a mistake.* We fear failure because we fear the misery we heap on ourselves when we make a simple mistake. Blaming, shaming, beating ourselves up . . . it's no fun! Procrastinating may keep us stuck, but it feels like a relief by comparison.

   By using Tapping to release limiting beliefs around what failure means about and for ourselves, we can quiet our critical voice, and in the process, let go of the need for our critical voice and for procrastination.

3. *The story you tell yourself about what will happen if you fail.* We look into the future and tell ourselves horror stories of what will happen if we fail. No wonder we prefer procrastination! Using Tapping, we can let go of these fears, take on a less dramatic and more realistic view of failure, and move forward with more ease.

Let's begin processing and clearing these areas.

Step 1: Clearing Fear of Repeating Past Failures

Was there a moment in your past when you felt like you failed? This could be a big, obvious event or a time when you simply tried to speak your mind and felt shut down or embarrassed. If more than one come to mind, select the event that feels most intense right now.

Let's use Tapping to clear it.

First notice how much emotional intensity you experience when you focus on that event or time. When you think back on that time, did you feel like a total, complete failure (9 or 10 out of 10) or mostly a failure (7 or 8 out of 10). Go with your gut and give your feeling of failure a number of intensity on a scale of 0 to 10.

Take a deep breath.

Beginning with the Karate Chop point, start tapping as you tell the story of that failure. As you continue telling it, keep tapping through the points. Include as many details of your memory as possible. The more you can conjure up the event, how you felt, even your surroundings—sights, smells, sounds, and so on—the more powerful your clearing will be.

Continue tapping through the points for as many rounds as you need to experience relief:

Eyebrow . . . Side of Eye . . . Under Eye . . . Under Nose . . . Under Mouth . . . Collarbone . . . Under Arm . . . Top of Head . . .

Eyebrow . . . Side of Eye . . . Under Eye . . . Under Nose . . . Under Mouth . . . Collarbone . . . Under Arm . . . Top of Head . . .

Eyebrow . . . Side of Eye . . . Under Eye . . . Under Nose . . . Under Mouth . . . Collarbone . . . Under Arm . . . Top of Head . . .

When you're ready, rate how intensely that time or event evokes a sense of failure on a scale of 0 to 10. Keep tapping until you can retell the entire story, beginning to end, without feeling like you failed or feeling ashamed, fearful, sad, and so on.

Once you can look at that event simply as something that didn't work out as you'd hoped, you've successfully cleared it. At that point you can move forward wiser and more aware of what to do differently next time.

Refer to page 230 of the Appendix for an extended Tapping script on Releasing Fear from Past Failure.

Next let's look at anything recent, current, or ongoing that is making you feel like you've failed.

Step 2: Fear of Future Failure

If you will be irritated by every rub, how will you be polished?

— Rumi

My husband often tells me, "Stop trying to solve a problem that doesn't exist!" It's where I naturally go when I'm scared to take action. I try to think about every scenario and try to solve it. Of course, I then feel stuck, and in that moment, being stuck is helpful because if I don't try, I can't possibly fail, and that feels safer than failing. When I realize what I'm doing (or my husband points it out), I can step back and realize that I'm just scared. I can then tap on releasing my fear and feeling safe creating movement that supports me in getting unstuck.

Too often we create a big story around what will happen if we try something and fail. When we get clear on that story and use Tapping to release its negative emotional charge, we are no longer stuck in that fear. Instead, we can trust in our dreams and take positive action toward them.

With Tapping, our goal is to change the way we react to disappointment, not to never feel disappointed again.

Focus on something that you would like to do or make or have happen in your future. When you think about it, ask yourself, *What story do I tell myself about what will happen if I try and fail?*

Next ask yourself, *How is procrastination keeping me safe? Is it allowing me to avoid failure? Is it protecting me from the disappointment I feel when I fail? Is it protecting me from the harsh way I treat myself when I make a mistake?*

Tune in to your feelings surrounding the possibility of trying something and failing, and rate their intensity on a scale from 0 to 10.

Note: This is a sample Tapping script, with only one negative round and one positive. The complete, expanded script is in the Appendix on page 232.

Take a deep, cleansing breath.

Begin your tapping by focusing on the negative emotions you'd like to release.

Karate Chop (*repeat three times*): Even though I'm scared to try, I honor how I feel, and I give myself permission to release this fear.

Sample Negative Round:

Eyebrow: I'm scared to try

Side of Eye: What if I fail?

Under Eye: What if I disappoint others?

Under Nose: What if I disappoint myself?

Under Mouth: I can't try

Collarbone: I might fail

Under Arm: And that's way too risky

Top of Head: It's better to not try at all

Sample Positive Round:

Eyebrow: I've been telling myself an old story that if I try and fail

Side of Eye: Then it means I'm not good enough

Under Eye: Then it means all is lost

Under Nose: I notice this irrational fear and belief

Under Mouth: And I replace it with reassurance

Collarbone: No matter what happens

Under Arm: I have my own back

Top of Head: No matter what happens, I'll be okay

Take a deep breath. Again rate the intensity of your fear of future failure on a scale of 0 to 10. Keep tapping until you feel the desired relief.

There is a famous question that shows up, it seems, in every single self-help book ever written: What would you do if you knew that you could not fail? But I've always seen it differently. I think the fiercest question of all is this one: What would you do even if you knew that you might very well fail? What do you love doing so much that the words failure and success essentially become irrelevant? What do you love even more than you love your own ego? How fierce is your trust in that love?

— Elizabeth Gilbert

Intuitive Procrastination

Occasionally, we may also fall into procrastination for a different reason—because moving forward, at least at that particular time, doesn't feel right. I call that *intuitive procrastination*.

When we listen to its hidden message, intuitive procrastination supports us in finding flow by showing us it's time to pause, time to rest and reset, as Mother Nature does each winter.

I experienced *intuitive procrastination* during the months following the release of my first book. At the time, I was longing for another big creative challenge to dig my teeth into. My initial answer was to move forward with my second book. When I found the project was stalling and I felt stuck, I had to dig deeper. *Am I stalling because I'm scared? What's the downside of moving forward on this project? What is this hesitation trying to tell me?*

By using Tapping to get quiet and listen to my procrastination, I noticed that something about diving into my second book didn't feel right. In that quiet, calm state, we can access our intuitive procrastination. Without it, we struggle to distinguish between a gut feeling that says "Now is not the time" and the fear that leads us to procrastinate. Once we get quiet, we can more easily hear what each instance of procrastination is trying to tell us.

At that particular time in life, I realized that I was seeking creative expression, but not necessarily through a second book. That knowing allowed me to begin exploring other forms of creative self-expression. I eventually decided to launch my podcast, *Adventures in Happiness*. That podcast provided the creative fulfillment I was yearning for, and it also fit more easily into the ups and downs I was experiencing in my life at the time (I had moved across country and was still settling in). That podcast has since allowed me to learn from dozens of inspiring experts, and of course, led me many months later to write my second book, which is the one you now hold in your hands.

If you feel like you might be experiencing *intuitive procrastination*, ask yourself, *What feeling am I yearning for?* Once you have that answer, you can search for a different way to feel that desired feeling.

When Ease Needs to Come First

Another reason we procrastinate is because we experience discomfort and put ourselves on trial for procrastinating, judging ourselves way too harshly.

That was the case with Joanne, a client I was working with who wanted to lose weight. She'd begun our session bemoaning her habit of procrastinating on adopting healthier lifestyle habits. When I asked her to share more, she explained that her mother had just passed away. She was taking care of all the funeral planning and estate issues while hosting friends and family who had come to pay their respects. Food was everywhere, and she'd been putting off Tapping, overindulging in unhealthy treats, and skipping the daily workouts she'd promised herself.

I was silent for a brief moment, overwhelmed just hearing all that she had on her plate. "Joanne," I replied, "is there any chance you're being too hard on yourself? You've got a *lot* going on right now. I'm just wondering if this is the time to focus on weight loss."

She was silent.

"Your mom just passed away," I continued. "You've got guests staying with you. All the load is falling on you. Let's change the focus from achieving something to finding more comfort during this difficult time."

Joanne hesitated before conceding that it was possible. We did some Tapping on how overwhelmed she was feeling about her mom's passing, her houseguests, the funeral, and the endless to-dos that all those things required. By the time our session was over, she agreed to focus more on being kind to herself, rather than on losing weight. "That will come," I told her. "Just give yourself a break right now."

We live in a culture that's so focused on doing and achieving that we often forget to notice one thing—we're human. Instead of acknowledging our basic human limits, we take on superhuman to-do lists and then call ourselves procrastinators because we didn't get it all done. Like Joanne, we expect ourselves to handle it all, even when some unexpected event—an injury, illness, divorce, losing a loved one, and more—derails us.

We do this because, especially when change is forced upon us, we seek certainty, safety, and stability. When life feels tumultuous, we're more easily lulled into believing that conquering our gargantuan to-do lists will make uncertainty feel less uncertain. Getting it all done, we tell ourselves, will make it *seem* like we're in control.

The problem is, of course, that we overwhelm ourselves with so many tasks that we're setting ourselves up for failure. We pile so much on our plates that getting stuck is almost inevitable. That creates more uncertainty, rather than less. Also, because we're worn down and beating up on ourselves, we have an even harder time dealing with the uncertainty we're already facing.

As we dive deeper into what procrastination really is, let me say this:

Setting the bar of what's "enough" too high, as Joanne did, is not procrastination. It's being human.

If you feel like you've gotten stuck in procrastination, first ask yourself, *Am I procrastinating or asking too much of myself?*

One hallmark of setting the bar too high is that there's a time limit on whatever peak-intensity circumstances we're facing. Once those circumstances ease, we're able to resume incremental progress at a reasonable pace. However, if we're still avoiding those same tasks months or years afterward, we have most likely slipped from setting the bar too high into procrastinating.

Another driving force behind procrastination is the fear of success. It can sound odd at first, but it's a lot more common than most of us realize.

The Fear of Success

Sometimes we're scared to even try to realize our dreams because success doesn't feel safe. That's because it requires us to shine. To be successful we have to put ourselves out there and, in the process, risk being ridiculed and rejected.

Since I was a drama fixer and never wanted to disappoint others, being successful felt overwhelming. The more successful you are, the more opportunities present themselves, and if you don't know how to say no, that success can feel terrifying. Speeding down a highway in a nice car isn't fun if you suddenly realize you don't have brakes! Every day I get interview requests, and every day I have to say no to some of them, which means every day I'm disappointing someone. But if I said yes to every opportunity, then I wouldn't have time for my own passions. This is just one way success can be scary: we fear it won't be sustainable or there will be negative consequences, like disappointing others.

To avoid feeling that pain, we resort to procrastination, again as a way of protecting ourselves. When we procrastinate, we don't attract as much attention. We can continue playing small and receive less feedback, rather than more.

Let's use Tapping to begin releasing that fear now.

Letting Go of Limitations

To begin lessening fear around success, let's first do some general Tapping on it.

Rate how afraid you feel when you envision achieving success in whatever way or part of your life where you most desire it. Focus on what that success will feel like. Then ask yourself, *What will I have to give up to experience that success? What feels uncomfortable and unsafe about realizing this kind of success?* On a scale of 0 to 10, how afraid are you of achieving and maintaining that success, or of suffering from any negative consequences you envision coming from that success?

Note: This is a sample Tapping script, with only one negative round and one positive. The complete, expanded script is in the Appendix on page 235.

Take a deep, cleansing breath.

We'll begin by tapping on your Karate Chop point.

Begin tapping on the fear you feel.

Karate Chop (*repeat three times*): Even though I'm scared to try because I might succeed, and then I'll have to shine my light in the world, I deeply and completely love and accept myself.

Sample Negative Round:

Eyebrow: I'm scared I'll succeed

Side of Eye: If I succeed, I'll have to shine

Under Eye: What if I'm unworthy?

Under Nose: What if I'm a fraud?

Under Mouth: I'm scared to be seen at that level

Collarbone: I'm scared I'll succeed

Under Arm: It feels too risky

Top of Head: It's better to not try at all

Sample Positive Round:

Eyebrow: I've been telling myself an old story that I'm unworthy of success

Side of Eye: That it's easier not to try

Under Eye: I am safe being seen

Under Nose: I'm safe shining my light in the world

Under Mouth: I am worthy of the success I desire

Collarbone: Releasing this fear of success now

Under Arm: I can put time and energy into my own success

Top of Head: And know that I'm safe and worthy, always

Take a deep breath. Rate how intense your fear of success feels now on a scale of 0 to 10. Keep tapping until you experience the desired relief.

Tapping on Past Success

Similar to releasing fear of failure, it can be helpful to use Tapping to let go of negative emotions and limiting beliefs from past and future success you've experienced, seen, or heard about.

Note: These questions are designed to help you get clear on whether you have any blocks around success. Write down anything that comes up as you go through them.

Looking first at past success, ask yourself:

- *Was there a time in my past when I succeeded and something bad happened?*
  For example, one client remembered coming home and telling her mom about a good grade she'd gotten. Her mom told her to "stop bragging" because she was making her sister feel bad. That client quickly took on the belief that her success was shameful because it would make others feel badly. Decades later, she realized she'd been operating on the belief that her success is shameful ever since her mom said that.

- *When I imagine myself being successful in the future, what comes to mind as the downside(s)?*
  Let's say you imagine getting the promotion or dream job you've always wanted. You then realize that your co-workers would resent you if you were in a leadership position and they weren't. They may then talk about you behind your back and exclude you from their social outings. In that sense playing small, which in this example means staying in your current job, feels safer than creating the change you desire.

Decisions, Decisions, Always More Decisions

Sometimes what keeps us stuck in procrastination is having to make decisions that we don't want to make or aren't sure how to make. Here are some powerful decision-making tips:

- *Reinforce your faith in yourself and your journey.*
  When we feel immense pressure around making a choice, we prefer not to make a decision rather than to make the wrong one. No amount of Tapping, research, or meditation will ensure that you're making a "perfect" choice. There is no crystal ball that can predict your future. Using Tapping to release the pressure reminds you that no matter what happens, you'll be okay. You then have the freedom to make a decision. Keep in mind, very few things in life are permanent. If you don't

like the choice you've made, you can change your mind. Have faith that even a seemingly wrong decision can eventually lead you to something better than you first imagined.

- *Listen to the whispers of your intuition by giving yourself quiet time.*
  You can be driving in the car without music or talking, doing mindless household chores, meditating, taking a nature walk, or something similar. However and wherever you take your quiet time is less important than taking it. This time gives you a chance to connect with your inner wisdom, and that, most of all, will help to guide you.

- *Notice the difference between what you think and what someone else thinks.*
  Often we know what feels right for us but we struggle to admit it to ourselves because we think it may conflict with what others think. A great way to gain clarity on which decision feels right to *you* is by asking yourself, *If no one else's opinion mattered, what decision would I make?*

- *Check in with yourself and ask, Is now the time to make this decision?*
  Procrastinating on a decision may be your intuition telling you to slow down and wait. We often pressure ourselves to make a decision because we feel impatient and hope to avoid the uncertainty. If you tap on your fear and the answer still isn't clear, then what you need is more time and space.

- *Make decisions from a place of abundance, not lack.*
  When we make decisions from a place of fear and lack, we focus on what we're losing, rather than remembering that letting go of what we have may make space for new options that are better suited to our needs and desires. By opening up to abundance and possibility, we can make more empowered and fulfilling decisions.

Now that we've looked at fear-based procrastination, let's look at one final reason we procrastinate—because we're avoiding what I call "the suck."

Accepting "The Suck"

After filling my water bottle, I turned to walk out of the kitchen and back to my cozy little home office. That's when I saw it—that all-too-familiar stack of wedding thank-you cards it had taken me a month to write.

I'd felt so relieved and proud of myself for finishing them. Our wedding had been better than my dreams, but I was ready to return to normal life. Sending those cards was my last wedding-related to-do.

Yet here I was, more than two weeks later, and there they still were—all 70 cards sealed and addressed, sitting on our kitchen counter. Not a single card had been mailed. It made sense, really, when you consider that the post office closes early. Granted, I do live in a small town, so it's not like I could blame my delay on a long drive. All I needed were stamps and a mailbox. It sounded so easy, but going and getting the stamps, affixing them, and putting the cards into a mailbox, well, it just hadn't yet happened.

Procrastination, ugh! I have a habit of doing that when it comes to mailing things. This time, though, I'd promised myself I wouldn't. Thanking all the people who had flown thousands of miles to our wedding was too important.

Yet here I was, staring at The Pile. Again.

For me, mailing things falls into the category I like to refer to as "the suck." It's just how I feel about mailing things. I don't enjoy it. I prefer to put it off. It's my personal version of the suck.

Let's be real, though—in order to achieve success in different parts of our lives, we sometimes need to do things that we don't enjoy. I happen to be writing this chapter in mid-April, smack in the middle of tax season. Doing taxes, for many of us, is the epitome of the suck. They have to get done, but few of us look forward to the work involved in doing them.

However you specifically define the suck, we all have things we have to do that we wish we didn't have to deal with!

When you're feeling tempted to procrastinate around accepting and completing the suck, Tapping can help to ground you in how amazing it will feel to have that task done and off your list.

To begin, notice how much dread you feel around accepting the suck. Give that dread a number of intensity on a scale of 0 to 10.

Note: This is a sample Tapping script, with only one negative round and one positive.

Take a deep, cleansing breath.

Begin by tapping on the Karate Chop point.

Karate Chop *(repeat three times)*: Even though I don't want to do this, it's no fun at all, I honor how I feel and I'm open to making this easier.

Sample Negative Round:

Eyebrow: This just "sucks"

Side of Eye: I wish I didn't have to do it

Under Eye: I keep putting it off

Under Nose: And I have so many other things I'd rather be doing

Under Mouth: It's the last thing I want to do

Collarbone: It's weighing on me

Under Arm: I wish I could make it just go away

Top of Head: I don't want to do this

Sample Positive Round:

Eyebrow: I acknowledge my resistance

Side of Eye: I acknowledge how uncomfortable it feels to start

Under Eye: I'm tired of fighting myself about it

Under Nose: I honor that I don't like to do this

Under Mouth: And allow myself to find small ways to feel more ease

Collarbone: I've been thinking about it so much

Under Arm: I allow myself to stop thinking

Top of Head: And simply take the first step

Continue tapping until you feel ready to accept and complete the suck. Getting it done and off your list will feel amazing! I experienced that very feeling on the way home from the post office, just the other day. So worth it!

Finding Comfort in Discomfort

Even after using Tapping on the underlying fears that lead us into procrastination, we may still feel some fear around taking action.

Barbara, who identified herself as a *drama shrinker* (as defined in Chapter 6), experienced some of her familiar old fears when she decided to take action on something she'd been putting off for months—having an honest conversation with her roommate about the clutter in their shared kitchen.

After using Tapping on the underlying cause of her procrastination—her fear that speaking up would cause a rift with her roommate—Barbara decided to speak up. She was so nervous that her voice shook, but because she'd tapped on her fears, she was able to explain how she was feeling. To Barbara's relief, her roommate was receptive. They made a plan together, and before long their kitchen was less cluttered and Barbara felt a lot more comfortable and confident in their apartment.

Daisha had a similar experience around making her first music album. Her intention was to send that album to well-known composers who had expressed interest in her music. For a year, however, Daisha procrastinated on creating her first recordings.

One day during a group call, Daisha did some Tapping on how overwhelming and scary making her own album sounded. After tapping, she felt relief and resolved to complete 10 takes of her music before going to bed. She proceeded to do exactly that. A few days later, she realized that she needed to tap again on her fear that her recordings wouldn't be good, as that fear was preventing her from listening to what she'd recorded. After tapping on that fear, she was able to listen to them and was thrilled to discover that she felt really good about her first recordings. During the months that followed, she worked with professionals to get her album ready for production. When I last spoke with Daisha, she had just delivered her first shipment of the album to the composers who had requested it.

Most important of all, she'd found a new way forward. As she said, "Thanks to Tapping, I've realized that you don't have to be good to go, you just have to take one step forward." Rather than needing to "heal" her procrastination fully, she understood that she could use Tapping to move forward whenever she noticed herself falling back into procrastination.

Both Barbara and Daisha still felt afraid of taking action, but thanks to Tapping, they were both able to move forward anyway. If, even after tapping, you feel some fear or nervousness around taking action, know that there's no need to worry. That's normal! I love public speaking, but feel nervous every time I go on stage. Once I start speaking, I quickly find my flow and feel calm and present. I often have a similar experience before working on a chapter. Before I begin, I feel that same nervous anticipation, even self-doubt, because I'm never sure if things will go as planned. Once I get going, though, the process is a lot easier.

What Tapping does is provide clarity around which action to take and how to move into it. It also provides more ease and willingness around creating that movement in your life. That unto itself is huge—each little (and big) step forward makes all the difference!

Time for the End-of-Chapter Tapping Meditation!

What are you ready to move forward on? Take a few moments now to use the Chapter 9 Tapping Meditation to create that movement with more clarity and ease. Remember, if tapping on your discomfort doesn't ease you into action, it's probably time to look deeper and notice any fears holding you back.

CHAPTER 9 TAPPING MEDITATION: CLEARING FRUSTRATION AND HEARING THE WISDOM OF YOUR PROCRASTINATION

At this moment, how intense does your struggle with procrastination feel? How frustrated are you? Rate the emotional intensity of that struggle on a scale of 0 to 10.

Take a deep breath.

Begin tapping on the Karate Chop point.

Karate Chop *(repeat three times)*: Even though I'm so frustrated with myself for procrastinating, I accept myself and I'm open to finding more clarity and ease.

Eyebrow: I've been thinking about "it" for so long

Side of Eye: But I keep putting it off

Under Eye: It's hard to find the time

Under Nose: I know I should have figured this out by now

Under Mouth: I should be further along by now

Collarbone: All these feelings around this procrastination

Under Arm: All this frustration

Top of Head: All of this disappointment

Eyebrow: All these judgments I have

Side of Eye: It seems easier for everyone else

Under Eye: I've struggled with procrastination for so long

Under Nose: I try to bully myself to take action

Under Mouth: If I'm frustrated with myself for procrastinating

Collarbone: Then I'll be able to move forward

Under Arm: Is that really true?

Top of Head: I'm open to a new way

Eyebrow: I honor this struggle

Side of Eye: I honor how I feel

Under Eye: And I give myself permission to relax

Under Nose: Even though I've been procrastinating

Under Mouth: I love, accept, and forgive myself

Collarbone: I'm open to the idea

Under Arm: That I may be exactly where I'm meant to be

Top of Head: I am on the verge of a breakthrough

Eyebrow: I am open to divine wisdom

Side of Eye: I replace my criticism with curiosity

Under Eye: I listen to the wisdom of my procrastination

Under Nose: Am I putting too much pressure on myself?

Under Mouth: Am I fearful?

Collarbone: I honor my unique experience

Under Arm: And I am open to making this easy

Top of Head: I've tried pushing myself for so long

Eyebrow: I now experience more flow

Side of Eye: It is safe to move forward with ease

Under Eye: I let go of the tension

Under Nose: And move at my own pace

Under Mouth: It's safe for me to try something new

Collarbone: As I start I find more ease

Under Arm: I feel pulled to do this

Top of Head: I honor this calling and take action with ease

Eyebrow: I no longer need to push myself

Side of Eye: Instead I feel pulled by my desires

Under Eye: Holding myself back has been exhausting

Under Nose: I give myself permission to let go

Under Mouth: And move forward

Collarbone: Now is the time

Under Arm: Now is my time

Top of Head: I'm further along than I realize

Take a deep, relaxing breath. Check in again on your frustration and other emotions you feel around procrastinating. Keep tapping until you experience the desired release.

IF you're waiting for that PERFECT someday, you're FOREVER putting your HAPPINESS on HOLD

Chapter 10

Every Step Counts

Hungry? Order food without getting up. Lonely? Make a call or send a text. Bored? Stream a movie, open an app, download a book, check social media. We live in a culture that's obsessed with instant gratification. We want to be able to do one thing and get an immediate result.

No matter how much is instantaneously accessible, the journey of life can only move *so* fast. We know this, yet with so much available to us so quickly, we forget. That's when taking the little steps to realize a larger vision can feel frustrating, even pointless.

We need to get to a place where we can continually take action and not feel disappointed or like we're failing when the desired outcome doesn't happen overnight. When it comes to realizing a larger vision, it's taking one step after another that makes all the difference.

In this chapter, we'll take a fresh look at what holds us back, and we'll use Tapping to add joy back into the big and little steps we take from one day to the next. First, though, let's pause and consider how taking those steps supports us in creating lasting change and finding flow.

Consistency and Flow

Change and flow, by nature, require movement. We can't remain perpetually still and create change or be in flow. We have to take action, and as we've seen, just as a plant grows toward sunshine, we have to be moving toward *something*.

Our vision, the sum of our intentions, acts as the sunlight we grow toward. That vision nurtures and inspires us. It motivates us to try things, even when those things are outside our comfort zones. Our vision is *why* we create movement in our lives.

By taking action steps, we create positive momentum toward that vision. We can then grow, sprout new buds, find new sources of nourishment, and manifest new branches we never knew we were capable of creating.

It's a self-perpetuating cycle that supports lasting change, as well as fulfillment, joy, and flow. So why do we struggle so often with taking those steps that are essential to creating lasting change? Next we'll look at some of the blocks we encounter in this part of the process.

The Perfection Trap

One of the most common blocks to practicing consistency often surprises people. It's not schedule overload or lack of motivation or energy. It's perfectionism.

We start feeling motivated, but if we have one small slipup in our effort to be consistent, we chalk it up as failure. We treat ourselves so harshly for each and every mistake we make that it becomes easier not to try at all.

This can also manifest as a "go big or go home" way of thinking. One client learned that saying from her father. As an adult, she found herself stalling on taking action because her actions wouldn't measure up to her all-or-nothing standards.

Instead of accepting our imperfections from a place of love and appreciation, we avoid taking consistent, positive action because we think taking fewer chances will mean less risk of disappointing others or ourselves. While this may seem to solve the problem at first, eventually we have to face the fact that we still feel just as afraid. We're also still just as self-critical as we've always been.

In other words, playing small because we can't live up to perfectionist standards eventually gets us stuck. One client noticed this pattern in her daily routine. Most mornings she would struggle to get going on her projects. There were always several for her to focus on, but she hesitated to move forward on any of them because she knew she couldn't live up to her "perfect" standards.

One of the biggest reasons we cling to this desire to do things perfectly is that we hope to avoid criticism. We think if it's perfect, we won't have to face other people's negative opinions. The problem is, there are eight billion people on this planet, and everyone on the Internet has an opinion. In this day and age, criticism is unavoidable. Even by striving to create something so perfect that everyone loves it, we increase the chances that we'll give up too soon or never finish what we start because it will never be perfect enough to be loved by all. As Elbert Hubbard famously said, "To avoid criticism, say nothing, do nothing, be nothing."

To create lasting change your focus can't be on avoiding criticism. It has to be on caring more about what *you* think than what other people think.

My brother Nick and I became acutely aware of how limiting the fear of criticism can be when we each became first-time authors. It was scary putting a book out in the world! As authors, it was impossible *not* to worry and wonder how our books, which we'd put so much of ourselves into, would be received.

To help ourselves overcome our fear of criticism, we began celebrating the first time each of our books got a one-star review on Amazon. It was our way of acknowledging that the more people read our books, the more likely those books were to also reach people who didn't resonate with them. By celebrating that first one-star review, we were allowing ourselves to accept that not everyone would love our books.

We eventually began sharing this funny ritual with friends who were also authors. As soon as their first one-star review would show up, we'd call them and take a few moments to celebrate their increased exposure. It felt ridiculous to celebrate a one-star review, but it was also incredibly freeing! When your fear of being criticized becomes a reality that you then live through, it's liberating. You move through your fear and realize that you're okay, even after what you've created has been criticized.

For Nick and me, as well as our friends, celebrating that first one-star review has been a great way to notice how normal it is to fear the disappointment we all feel when our hopes and expectations aren't met. At that point, our fear of criticism and failure doesn't feel like such a big deal. Instead, it becomes a natural part of the process. We can move through our fear, rather than let it take hold of us and keep us stuck.

WHEN IT COMES TO PERFECTIONISM, MANY OF US ARE STRUGGLING!

I'm so passionate about how perfectionism keeps us from taking consistent action that I recently posted a Facebook Live video about the topic. Here are a few of the comments I received:

- "Hi! The video really did resonate with me. I have a new position at work and am the lead on a new project with a deadline this week. I have been working so hard to get everything just right and have found myself cranky and overwhelmed to the point of procrastination. Which, of course, only stresses me out more. After the tapping yesterday, I was able to clear my head and got a whole bunch more done. I even slept better last night and have been way more productive today!"

- "Jessica, you addressed my boogie man! Thank you! I am always so concerned about doing a good job that I overwhelm myself with fear and worry. I don't know why, because I always get 'it' done on time and get it done well. I want to be able to get it done well without the stress, worry, and panic into which I often sink. I want to enjoy the process with comfort and confidence and expect the best outcome. Thank you for your generosity!"

- "This helped so much! I am working on two really important projects right now and I didn't even realize that this was the issue. THANK YOU!"

When we struggle with perfectionism, putting off action steps feels easier. Our inability to be consistent comes from masked fear. We fear not being able to live up to our own harsh standards, so we try, but only occasionally. We prefer not to create movement on a regular basis because then we can avoid the criticism we assume will come when we finish things and release them into the world.

Savor Every Little Success

Another important way to overcome perfectionism that keeps us from taking action is by savoring each and every success.

Each step forward matters. Each time you follow through counts. Savor every single time you practice consistency, every time you take action, including when the results of your action *don't* meet your expectations.

Every time you take action and celebrate the small step, you are reaffirming to your primitive brain that it is safe to take consistent action. When you allow yourself to feel pride and joy for every step forward, you are conditioning yourself to enjoy the process of moving forward consistently. The better each action you take feels, the easier it is to continue taking steps forward.

It's through taking action that we create lasting change, even when our actions are imperfect.

Better than "Perfect"

Even after years of cultivating awareness around how perfectionism can interfere with consistency, I still struggle sometimes. To remind me where to focus my energy, every time I'm starting a new project, I read and sometimes tap through this affirmation, which I wrote in my journals years ago:

I easily release my need for perfection by trusting that what I create in the moment is divine.

This affirmation reminds me that creating anything takes courage and trust. When I can have more trust in my own journey, I can see that where I am and what I created in that moment is divine; it's what I am meant to do. When I take this approach, I can consistently release my work into the world, knowing that it captured a moment in time and that I am still growing and evolving.

This same idea also helps me through the trial and error process that happens when we're consistently creating movement toward our dreams. I experienced that process prior to writing this book.

When I was first inspired to create a course around finding your flow, I envisioned it as a three-day journey. Feeling excited to share the techniques that have worked so well for me, I recorded a course that I was really excited about. After creating it, I shared it with friends and colleagues and got very mixed feedback.

Some liked the course, others really didn't. Once I'd processed the different reactions, I realized one of the problems was the structure I'd created. By trying to pack the content into three days, I'd condensed it too much. Several weeks later, after reconfiguring and editing the structure and content, I recorded it as a seven-week course that ended up helping others rediscover their flow in a whole new way. That seven-week course inspired this book.

None of that ever would have happened if I hadn't recorded the three-day course that got canned. Although I didn't realize it at the time, that three-day course was a seedling I planted that would bear fruit—but not until months later. If I'd gotten stuck in "failing" at creating that three-day course, I wouldn't have been able to flow toward the seven-week course or get the opportunity to write this book.

Experiences like this one have taught me repeatedly over the years that done is better than perfect. Even though it still feels scary sometimes, getting work out in the world is more important than being perfect or doing perfect work. If I wait for "perfect," I'll get stuck again. I'd rather take consistent action and flow through trial and error than feel paralyzed because I'm striving for a goal—aka perfection—that's impossible to achieve.

I have also learned to befriend my perfectionism in another way. Since I do care so much about doing the best work I can do, I tend to be very detail-oriented, double- and triple-checking work before it's released. As long as I keep it under control, that attention to detail often works in my favor. I hold myself to a higher standard, which can and does help me produce better work.

How Is Perfectionism Affecting Your Consistency?

Do you often hold yourself to a higher standard than you hold others to? Do you expect yourself to be perfect, say perfect things, do perfect work? Do you tend to brush off your accomplishments or avoid sharing them with others? What do you tend to say to yourself when something doesn't work out as you planned?

Let's take a closer look at how perfectionism may be affecting your ability to consistently create movement that supports you in creating lasting change and realizing your vision.

Do you feel like you have to be perfect? Where did this belief come from?

For example, you might realize, *I was punished for not getting perfect grades. I was yelled at for not performing well enough in sports, music, and so on.*

Think about putting something out in the world that you've judged as *not* good enough. When you imagine that, how do you feel? In your answer name one primary emotion you feel, such as panic, fear, shame, regret, or the like.

"I Must Be Perfect to Avoid Criticism"

An unhealthy fear of criticism often comes from an unhealed event in the past that caused us pain. Hoping to avoid feeling that pain again, we resolve to work hard at being perfect. Since perfection is unattainable, however, we end up causing ourselves additional pain.

After growing up in a highly critical family, one client realized she'd learned how to berate and belittle herself for every tiny misstep. Something as simple as overwatering her plants would lead her into harsh self-critique. However, after tapping on her perfectionism by focusing on what she says to herself when she makes a mistake and reminding herself of the following affirmation, she was able to quiet her critical voice and experience more self-compassion and flow:

I seek progress, not perfection. I celebrate every step forward.

Once we address the original pain that is pushing us toward perfectionism, we realize criticism can't really harm us. That's when we can form a healthier relationship with self-criticism and begin to release the belief that we need to be perfect. In that process we regain the freedom to consistently try new things and experiment, instead of being restricted by fear of making mistakes.

Let's do some general Tapping to pinpoint an event that contributed to your perfectionism.

Note: This is a sample Tapping script, with only one negative round and one positive. The complete, expanded script is in the Appendix on page 238.

Take a deep breath.

Begin by tapping on the Karate Chop point.

Karate Chop (*repeat three times*): Even though I learned as a child that I must be perfect in order to avoid being criticized, I honor my experience and accept myself.

Sample Negative Round:

Eyebrow: Somewhere in my past

Side of Eye: I picked up the idea

Under Eye: That I must be perfect

Under Nose: In order to deserve love

Under Mouth: Somewhere in my past

Collarbone: I picked up the idea

Under Arm: That I must be perfect

Top of Head: In order to avoid being criticized

Take a deep breath. After doing a few rounds of Tapping, pause and reflect.

Was there an event in the past where you learned you had to be perfect in order to be loved? Was there an event where you were criticized, and you vowed to be perfect in order to avoid that pain?

If an event comes to mind, before moving on with this Tapping script, take some time to tap on your own, using words to describe what happened and how you felt (sadness, shame, anger, and so on).

Note: If the event feels too painful, pretend that event is a movie. Give that movie a title—it can be as simple as *That Time I Was Humiliated*—and tap while simply saying that movie title until you feel more at ease with moving forward with more specifics.

If a particular event doesn't come up, that's okay too. Spend some time tapping on the fears that you currently feel, and then continue tapping when you are ready.

Sample Positive Round:

Eyebrow: All this time I was just trying to protect myself

Side of Eye: I wasn't following through on things

Under Eye: For a fear that it wouldn't be perfect

Under Nose: Fear that imperfection would cause me pain

Under Mouth: I was doing the best I could

Collarbone: I was just trying to protect myself

Under Arm: As I see this pattern clearly

Top of Head: I experience deep compassion for myself

Take a deep breath. Continue tapping until you feel the desired relief.

TIPS FOR MANAGING PERFECTIONISM

- *Embrace that life is a journey. There is no "finish line," no "someday" when life will be perfect.*

- Being a perfectionist can cause us to get stuck in in a "finish line" or "someday" mentality. For example, you may think things like, *Once I lose weight, life will be amazing,* or *One day I'll have enough money, and everything will be perfect.*

- This way of thinking steals the joy available to us in the present moment. We may one day have more money, and we may also lose weight, but by then we'll have a different "finish line," a new "someday" we want to reach.

- Life is a journey, and we're constantly growing and evolving. If we're always waiting for "that perfect someday," we're forever putting our joy on hold.

- *Find the bright side of your challenges.*

- We're taught to fear challenges, even though they're often our biggest and best opportunities in life. Obstacles come into our lives to be healed. Sometimes that takes time, which is why we get stuck in limiting patterns.

- Instead of bemoaning those patterns, try getting curious instead. By raising your awareness about why a pattern has been recurring in your life, you become better equipped to heal it and redirect your life in a more fulfilling direction.

- Let joy in every day.

- Put on your favorite song and dance. Grab an adult coloring book and let your imagination lead the way. Take a walk in the rain. Notice how the sunlight filters through the trees or between buildings. Savor your favorite tea or smoothie.

- Whatever lights you up on a given day, take a few minutes out and let yourself really feel the joy it brings. Making a point of feeling more joy every day can help you feel more refreshed and less self-critical.

Giving Meaning to the Process

Did you notice in Chapter 5 that when you gave meaning to clearing clutter by using a mantra, the task you'd been dreading and avoiding felt easier? When you say something like "As I clean out the back of my car, I travel smoothly through life," the whole experience feels different. You are focusing on a meaningful outcome.

I used to struggle with being consistent with my workouts. As I began to look deeper at why I kept stopping and restarting, I realized I had given exercise a disempowering meaning; for years I'd been telling myself that exercise was my punishment for being fat.

When I asked friends who were consistent with exercise and looked forward to working out why they were able to be consistent, none ever replied, "I exercise regularly because I hate my body and feel desperate to change it."

My friend Erin Stutland, a fitness expert and coach, has a powerful mantra that has helped me give exercise a new meaning. Her mantra is "Movement in my body means movement in my life." Now I know that moving my body is about my spirit as much as it is about my body. With this more empowering meaning in my mind, exercise became easier to do.

If it's not pleasurable, it's not sustainable.

When we assign meaning to the process of being consistent in any part of our lives, we transform something we've dreaded into a source of mental, emotional, and physical nourishment. We add ease and flow to the experience of taking consistent action.

Whatever task or part of your life where you're seeking more consistency, try adding more meaning and joy to the process.

Let's do some Tapping on feeling centered where you are now.

First notice, when you think about taking consistent action, how intensely resistant—or impatient, dissatisfied, frustrated—you feel on a scale of 0 to 10.

Note: This is a sample Tapping script, with only one negative round and one positive. The complete, expanded script is in the Appendix on page 241.

Take a deep breath and begin tapping.

Karate Chop *(repeat three times)*: Even though I'm feeling really unsure and impatient with where I am, I accept myself and choose to relax.

Sample Negative Round:

Eyebrow: I'm not where I should be

Side of Eye: It doesn't feel good

Under Eye: It feels like I'll never get where I want to be

Under Nose: Feeling impatient and unsure

Under Mouth: Not happy with where I am now

Collarbone: I should be farther along

Under Arm: All this impatience

Top of Head: It's stealing my joy

Sample Positive Round:

Eyebrow: Maybe everything is unfolding as it should

Side of Eye: I trust that things are lining up

Under Eye: I could quit now

Under Nose: Or move forward with trust

Under Mouth: Every person I look up to

Collarbone: Has faced moments of doubt and impatience

Under Arm: Maybe this moment

Top of Head: Is part of a greater story

Take a deep breath. Rate your impatience again on a scale of 0 to 10. Keep tapping until you feel the desired level of peace.

STILL STRUGGLING WITH CONSISTENCY? THAT'S OKAY.

We often give our struggles a deeper meaning without noticing. Rather than accepting struggle as a natural part of our journey, we tell ourselves that our struggles mean that we're not good enough. We let our critical voice take over when self-acceptance would be far more empowering.

Through experience and practice, successful people learn to view difficulties as normal parts of any process. Challenges can then become learning opportunities that allow them to realize success faster and better than they originally envisioned.

A powerful way to remind yourself of this is by writing the end of your story now.

First think about someone who inspires you. It could be a friend or family member, or a celebrity or historical figure. Ask yourself, *What inspires me about this person's story? Does she or he inspire me because she or he faced no challenges?* Of course not! We are inspired by how people respond to difficult moments in their lives.

Every great story includes one, or several, pivotal moments when self-actualization and whatever kind of success the person is seeking seems impossible. It's through persevering through those struggles that they discover what they're truly capable of. They become the heroes of their own story *because of* the challenges and obstacles they encounter.

Now you'll apply that same story structure to your own experiences. Imagine yourself in the future, looking back on the journey that led to your realizing your vision. Imagine looking back on all you've overcome, how many times you almost gave up, and how overjoyed and grateful you are that you persevered in spite of those challenges.

Write your larger story now, keeping in mind that your present experience is merely one short chapter of your much larger and greater journey. As you write from the vantage point of your future self, dwell in the gratitude you feel for the challenges you overcame, and how good your future self feels about not giving up.

Simple, Small Action Steps

People are often surprised by how *good* it feels to take action toward their vision. Even when we start out wanting to cross that theoretical finish line, once we're in flow, by taking action toward a vision, we discover that the process is *really* fun. That's because we're no longer stuck in fear, dread, or worry. We're doing it! We're moving our lives in positive new directions. It's incredibly rewarding to go to bed each night and wake up each morning knowing that you're no longer sitting on the sidelines. You're actively navigating your life toward your desires. It feels *amazing*.

So let's get started!

Pick one thing that you want to be more consistent with and schedule the action.

Then ask yourself, "How can I make this easier?"

For example, you might ask for support or schedule the task as an appointment on your calendar. It might also mean playing your favorite music or lighting a candle. Whatever supports you in *feeling* good as you take that action and create that movement, add it to your action step.

Time for the End-of-Chapter Tapping Meditation!

In the last chapter, we'll discuss one of the most important elements of any journey, and that's cultivating the faith and trust we need to move forward in the face of life's many unknowns.

First, make sure to complete the Chapter 10 Tapping Meditation.

CHAPTER 10 TAPPING MEDITATION: EASING INTO CONSISTENCY

Sometimes the scariest thing to do is simply to start.

Maybe it's a project that you care so much about that you freeze in fear that it won't be good enough.

Or maybe it's something you would love to get done, but the task itself feels tedious.

Let's use Tapping to find more ease around getting started.

Start by noticing your resistance to taking action on a project. The resistance may show up as tension in your body, like a knot in your stomach or a tightness in your throat. Notice any physical sensation and rate its intensity on a scale of 0 to 10.

Let's begin with a deep breath.

Karate Chop (*repeat three times*): Even though I'm resisting working on this project, and it's so easy to put this off, I accept myself and am open to getting started with ease.

Eyebrow: This task has been weighing on me

Side of Eye: Part of me wants to work on it

Under Eye: And part of me is scared

Under Nose: Part of me wants to get this finished

Under Mouth: And part of me is resistant

Collarbone: It's not an easy task

Under Arm: It often feels overwhelming

Top of Head: All this pressure that I feel

Eyebrow: This project feels hard

Side of Eye: It feels tedious

Under Eye: And I've been beating myself up

Under Nose: I should be further along by now

Under Mouth: This should already be done

Collarbone: I acknowledge the pressure I feel

Under Arm: I've been trying to push myself to start

Top of Head: And it hasn't been working

Eyebrow: I'm open to a new way

Side of Eye: I acknowledge my fear

Under Eye: And allow myself to relax

Under Nose: I acknowledge the pressure I put on myself

Under Mouth: And I'm open to experiencing more ease

Collarbone: I release the need to do it perfectly

Under Arm: I give myself the freedom

Top of Head: To simply get started and experiment

Eyebrow: I don't need to know all the answers now

Side of Eye: I release my expectations

Under Eye: And simply start

Under Nose: I am flexible

Under Mouth: I am resourceful

Collarbone: I can lose myself in this project

Under Arm: I am present and calm

Top of Head: It feels so good to allow myself to start

Eyebrow: All this nervousness

Side of Eye: Turns into excited anticipation

Under Eye: I am ready

Under Nose: I give myself permission to experiment

Under Mouth: I move at my own pace

Collarbone: I honor the journey I'm on

Under Arm: I'm stepping out of my comfort zone

Top of Head: And it's uncomfortable

Eyebrow: I can be a little nervous

Side of Eye: And really, really ready

Under Eye: I am led forward

Under Nose: By courage and faith

Under Mouth: It's safe to get started

Collarbone: It's safe to experiment

Under Arm: I take it one step at a time

Top of Head: It feels so good to take action. I got this.

Take a deep breath and really exhale.

Notice how you feel about taking consistent action now. When we are doing something new or difficult, it's natural to feel a surge of energy. We choose whether that energy is fear or excited anticipation. When we let our mind and body know it's safe to try we will experience more ease around taking action.

Chapter 11

Trusting Life

I stood at the threshold, my stomach in knots. Just like that, when I least expected it, my dream had been swept away.

"I'm so sorry, Jess," I heard my brother Nick say in a voice tinged with concern. He paused, hoping for a reply. I grabbed the doorframe to steady myself, not yet able to speak. Disappointment had hit me like a punch in the gut.

In that moment, I had no clue what a huge blessing this turn of events would become. Right then and there, I had no idea that my life would transform in amazing ways specifically *because of* the hidden gifts in this moment. All I knew then was that I had a choice. I could make the best of this, or I could retreat. Most of me wanted to turn around and walk away, if only to have a good cry.

I had spent weeks researching and preparing for this interview. I had told friends and family about it, written and edited list after list of the questions I'd ask. I'd even bought a new dress.

For weeks, this interview had felt like an indication that my hard work and patience were finally paying off. Yet somehow, here I was on what was supposed to be my big day, being told that my big interview had been eliminated.

I took a few breaths, looked up at Nick, and nodded. "Okay, let's go in." He breathed a quick sigh of relief and stepped aside so I could enter.

"Hello. It is *so* nice to meet you," I said, extending my hand as I gathered all my remaining strength into a big smile. I was in Louise Hay's home, face to face with my idol. Since the 1970s, long before self-help was widely recognized, Louise Hay's pioneering work about the connection between the mind and body has inspired millions to change their lives by changing their thoughts. Her book *You Can Heal Your Life* has sold over 30 million copies.

I immediately got to work, helping the filming crew set up. Just moments earlier, Louise had asked my brother Nick to conduct the interview instead of me. His first book would be published soon, and she wanted to support him. That cooled the sting considerably, but the fact remained that after weeks of preparation and anticipation, I was now just a film crew assistant.

I moved quickly around the room, connecting wires, repositioning lights, doing anything and everything to avoid thinking about what had just happened. "Jessica!" I suddenly heard from behind me. Shocked, I turned around. Louise was speaking to me. "Trust life," she said. Our eyes locked briefly. I nodded. *Trust life. Okay. Trust life*, I repeated to myself silently. For the first time since arriving, I took a deep breath. I returned to work, feeling a renewed sense of calm.

Ever since that day, Louise Hay's words have stayed with me.

Trust life.

In that moment and the many years since, her words have inspired me more times than I can remember. They have been my guiding light through dark times. Those two words she gave me that day have transformed my life more powerfully than I can express, and I will forever be grateful. Not a day goes by when I don't reap the rewards of her reminder to stay centered in my trust and faith, no matter what's happening or how it seems.

In this chapter, we'll look at one of the most essential elements of creating lasting change and staying in flow—nurturing that trust, or faith, in life. We'll also look at what happens when our faith seems insufficient to support us and use Tapping to feel safer during this ever-changing journey we're co-creating.

Bridging the Trust Gap

Your trust in life is the foundation of your flow. It's ultimately what will best support your growth and evolution, and your ability to realize the most fulfilling outcomes in your life. However, unlike a typical foundation, which has to exist first, before anything can be built on it, your trust in life can only solidify *as* you create movement in your life.

Your "faith foundation" is built little by little, over time and often as a by-product of experience. That means that you'll feel, at times, like you're on shaky ground. That's because your foundation—your trust in life—is being laid beneath your feet as you create movement, experience trial and error, and navigate success as well as disappointment.

Especially when we're stretching and growing toward a vision, creating and navigating change, our trust in life often gets tested. It's not always an easy experience to flow through. In fact, the uncertainty we experience at those times can lure us back into getting stuck.

When Our Trust Seems to Be on Trial

It's when we face disappointments that we most need to fall back on our trust, yet that's also when we tend to brush aside and resist our need to trust. This is particularly true when we've been trying really hard to do everything "right." When we are tapping, taking action, reading books, staying positive, and still we experience disappointment, it's easy to throw our hands up in the air. That's when we think, *This doesn't work!*

I experienced that kind of discontent soon after the release of my first book. Although I had a successful career, supportive family, and circle of supportive friends in New York City, I'd begun feeling the need for a fresh start. That little nudge inside me persisted, like an intuitive whisper I couldn't avoid. I finally resolved to follow it, sold half of my belongings, and weeks later moved across the country to California.

Instead of refreshment and renewal, what I found in California was crushing loneliness and a growing number of health challenges. Weeks after my move, unable to bear another bout of the intense abdominal pain that had been plaguing me, I drove myself to the emergency room. After being advised to admit myself immediately, I was forced to wait in the hospital.

Afraid and alone, I called a family friend, Dr. Christiane Northrup, ob-gyn and best-selling author of *Women's Bodies, Women's Wisdom*. She calmly told me what questions to ask the doctors, and then said something that I'll never forget:

"Jess, your pain is in your lower abdomen. That's the part of your body that represents home and belonging."

I burst into tears and confessed that I'd never felt so lost in my life.

Although I didn't end up needing surgery that day, I did go home to my apartment feeling more afraid and exhausted than I had felt in a very long time. My family and friends were in New York and Connecticut, and I was all alone, thousands of miles away, with no solutions in sight.

At trying times like these, we feel stuck, lost, unable to move our lives forward. As much as we try, we can't find the answers we need, and the only thing we can fall back on is trust.

What if the disappointment we feel is only there to redirect us toward something better? What if our fear, loneliness, and whatever else we feel at those times is actually there to strengthen our faith more deeply and wholly than we ever imagined possible?

During especially challenging times, we experience waves of doubt, so we first have to rely on our courage. We have to take action with blind faith, trusting that somehow, in ways we can't yet imagine, things will work out.

I'll say that again—to create lasting change and stay in flow, we sometimes have to be courageous and create movement in our lives, even when we feel too scared or like we're not yet ready.

Courage is what fuels us when our trust in life isn't yet strong enough to support whatever movement we're creating, or whatever vision we're growing toward. Courage is what takes us to that next level. It's what allows us to gain the experience that will eventually expand and strengthen our trust in life.

So while you need that "trust foundation" as keenly as a house needs its concrete foundation pad, you have to move toward your vision *while* your foundation is being tested. You have to keep creating movement even when the ground under your feet feels shaky and unstable.

One of the first ways we gather together the courage we need is by reinforcing our new relationship with change. That's because we're never done strengthening our relationship with change. The uncertainty inherent in change will always remain outside our basic human comfort zone. We can never stop noticing and nurturing how we relate to change. Instead, we must strive continually to experience deeper ease within change, to feel more peace with the unknown we're forever facing.

Finding Greater Ease within Change

As we've seen, the primitive brain will encourage us to resist change, even when it's change we desire. This bias against change exists even on a neurological level. Inside the brain, change actually *is* harder. Every time we have a new thought, the brain has to create a new neural pathway to support it.

Creating movement and change feels like a lot of work because in many ways it is. Change forces the brain to work overtime. Even after we've made significant progress with creating change, adopted healthier habits, and done extensive inner work, it sometimes feels easier to go back to our old ways. At those times, even the pattern of panic can seem easier than doing the hard work of creating movement and navigating the uncertainty of change.

Staying continually aware of how the brain is resisting change will keep you from getting stuck. When you catch your brain trying to scare you out of creating movement and making changes that feel too big and uncertain, too slow, or too challenging, you can sit back and say, "Ha! I caught you! I know you're trying to protect me. I'm here to remind you it's safe for me to change."

Of course, this is also where Tapping is so helpful, supporting us in creating a new, more balanced relationship with uncertainty and change, which then supports ease and flow.

Is Change Happening *to* You? Or *for* You?

To conclude every interview for my podcast, *Adventures in Happiness*, I ask this same question:

What's something that happened to you that at the time seem horrible but ended up being a great blessing?

So many of us can look back and recall a romance that led to heartbreak. At the time that ending felt like the worst possible outcome, but years later, we feel incredibly grateful that that particular relationship didn't work out.

At the end of my interview with him, Dr. Mike Dow, therapist and author, shared the story of his brother's rare brain disease. When Mike was 16 years old, he and his family stayed in Michigan, far from their home, so his brother could undergo a critical but high-risk surgery.

In Michigan, Mike's brother shared a room with a boy who was around eight years old. That boy had been in a car accident and was badly injured physically, as well as emotionally. That little boy's trauma planted a seed that has since led Mike to find his life's work as a therapist. As painful and scary as that time was, he's now grateful for how it inspired him to dedicate his life to helping others. His brother, too, along with their mother, has co-founded a nonprofit that supports stroke survivors.

When we look back on painful and trying times that have already become a blessing, it's easy to be grateful for the positive outcomes they've helped us realize. However, when we're in the midst of those challenges, we often feel like the change we're facing is happening *to* us, rather than *for* us. We don't feel open to the idea that one day a hidden blessing will appear.

When you're navigating an overwhelming amount of uncertainty, or working through disappointment from change you didn't desire, do you feel like the changes are happening *to* you or *for* you? Do you have faith that good will come out of a bad situation? Let's do some Tapping on that now.

Being Open to Hidden Blessings

Be very honest with yourself. When something unexpected and undesired happens that causes you pain or disappointment, do you feel like change is happening *to* you? Think of a relevant example and rate how intensely you feel that change happened *to* you on a scale of 0 to 10.

Note: This is a sample Tapping script, with only one negative round and one positive. The complete, expanded script is in the Appendix on page 244.

Take a deep breath.

Begin tapping on the Karate Chop point.

Karate Chop (*repeat three times*): Even though things aren't going as planned, I open to the idea that new light will come from this darkness.

Sample Negative Round:

Eyebrow: Things aren't going as planned

Side of Eye: So much is changing

Under Eye: And it's not the kind of change I wanted

Under Nose: I often feel powerless

Under Mouth: So much is going on

Collarbone: That feels outside of my control

Under Arm: And I'm going through a difficult time

Top of Head: I'm faced with a difficult situation

Sample Positive Round:

Eyebrow: I can feel disappointed and still have faith

Side of Eye: That one day this moment will be part

Under Eye: Of a greater story

Under Nose: One day I'll see clearly

Under Mouth: How change was happening

Collarbone: For my greater good

Under Arm: From this darkness

Top of Head: I am discovering my own light

Take a deep breath. Again rate how intensely you feel like this change has happened to you on a scale of 0 to 10. Keep tapping until you feel the desired release.

Fearful *and* Courageous

It's through navigating past, present, and future change cycles, as well as trial and error, with this greater awareness and self-acceptance that, over time, we develop more courage to create movement and change in our lives, and through that, resume our flow. Even if we still feel afraid, disappointed, and more, we know that we have gained enough courage and resilience to survive any pain we may encounter.

In other words, contrary to what many of us were taught, courage isn't fearlessness. It's daring to be vulnerable—to feel disappointment, rejection, and more—and then let it go so we can move forward, in spite of our fear of the unknown that lies ahead.

One Little Step at a Time

For weeks after my visit to the emergency room in California, I continued to experience intense abdominal pain. The doctors couldn't yet tell me that an ovarian cyst had burst or that my intestines were badly inflamed. Without those answers, all I could do was gather my courage and try to trust—that I'd come out of this eventually, that someday this would all make sense.

Without any understanding of why I was in such pain and had no energy, I resolved to do whatever possible to help my body heal. I went on a strict anti-inflammatory diet and got as much rest as my work schedule would allow. I sipped bone broth and avoided sugar.

I did everything I could to care for myself, yet often couldn't help wondering if my intuition had led me astray. I tapped frequently, and although I felt better each time I did, I still didn't feel well. I still wasn't healthy. I still didn't know why all of this was happening.

Eventually, I made a decision. Rather than seeking healing, which seemed like a daunting undertaking, I sought relief. Little by little, day by day, I did what I could to feel a little bit better physically, a little less stressed, a little more trusting.

Was I impatient? Absolutely. I'd often look up and say, "I trust this is all happening for my greater good, but can you *please* hurry up and show me why?" Then I made sure to redirect my focus toward having *more* moments of faith, however imperfect they felt. Weeks turned into months before the blessings of my health challenges began to reveal themselves. Because I was sick and didn't have the energy to pack up and move back to the East Coast, I remained in California longer than I wanted. That additional time out West allowed me to meet Lucas, a man who changed my world forever.

After I met him, the pain in my stomach disappeared along with my doubt. I finally understood why I was there. Life had led me to him. We were married on January 14, 2017.

Time for the End-of-Chapter Tapping Meditation!

Before we conclude our journey, make sure to complete the Chapter 11 Tapping Meditation.

CHAPTER 11 TAPPING MEDITATION: BUILDING FAITH AND TRUST

These positive Tapping rounds can be added to any previous script when you want to strengthen your faith in yourself and your path.

There is nothing to rate, so simply take a deep breath and begin tapping at the Eyebrow point.

Eyebrow: As I begin to relax

Side of Eye: It becomes easier to have faith

Under Eye: Faith in my unique journey

Under Nose: The people I admire the most

Under Mouth: Didn't have a "perfect" path

Collarbone: They were faced with disappointments

Under Arm: But they found the faith to move forward

Top of Head: That is why I admire them

Eyebrow: Maybe I can begin to admire myself

Side of Eye: For how far I've come

Under Eye: I've had the courage to look within

Under Nose: I've been proactive

Under Mouth: Maybe what I'm facing is exactly what I need

Collarbone: To recognize my power

Under Arm: Maybe I'm further along than I recognize

Top of Head: I begin to notice how things have worked in my favor

Eyebrow: The universe has my back

Side of Eye: I have my own back

Under Eye: As I feel this support

Under Nose: I begin to stand taller

Under Mouth: As I begin to acknowledge my blessings

Collarbone: I can move forward with more confidence

Under Arm: As I recognize how far I've already come

Top of Head: I give myself permission to move forward in faith

Eyebrow: I honor my spirit

Side of Eye: By allowing myself to experiment

Under Eye: I allow myself to try new things

Under Nose: I give myself permission to make a mistake

Under Mouth: I give myself permission to change my mind

Collarbone: I honor the process

Under Arm: As I experience more trust and faith

Top of Head: I find the joy in this journey

Eyebrow: I trust in life

Side of Eye: I trust in my unique journey

Under Eye: It's safe to have hope

Under Nose: I give myself permission to feel good

Under Mouth: I recognize all the times when I felt lost

Collarbone: And when I found my way

Under Arm: I am never alone

Top of Head: Life supports me

Take a deep breath. Keep tapping until these words feel true and inspiring.

CONCLUSION

I wish I could tell you you'll learn these tools, complete this journey once, create lasting change, and never get stuck again. I wish I could say you'll never again face challenges you don't feel ready to face or make decisions you don't later doubt.

But that's not how life works. You're not going to leap over this mountain and never look back. You'll eventually get stuck again. You'll eventually feel like you've lost your flow, your courage, your essential trust in life. You'll cycle through the pattern of panic, feel victimized by change or lack thereof, and be disappointed by how trials turn into errors. It's not your fault. It's not even a problem. It's life.

However, when we have a tool like Tapping and a journey like this one to return to, we can navigate those experiences in different ways. Rather than getting stuck and staying stuck, we can become aware more quickly of how we're feeling, and use these tools to move through our emotions, experiences, and limiting beliefs.

We can face our fears, accept our imperfections, and find the gifts in events that have caused us pain and disappointment. We don't have to panic anymore, or at least not for as long. We're not alone. We're not powerless. We have tools; we have a journey to fall back on, a community of like-minded souls we can reconnect with.

Rather than shaming and blaming ourselves for being "there," in that stuck place, we can congratulate ourselves on noticing and get busy moving beyond it. Months after taking my seven-week course on finding your flow, a student, Lake, wrote me to share her journey:

Hi Jessica!

It is not an exaggeration to say that prior to using Tapping, my life had been compelled by fear and not feeling good enough. Painful feelings from early childhood of not being safe, valued, or loved were triggered repeatedly well into adulthood. After years of healing work, I had gained an intellectual understanding about the core limiting beliefs I was holding on to, but still, they felt very true.

I have used Tapping daily for over a year now.

Prior to this daily practice, I unrealistically believed Tapping (and before that, talk therapy and other healing techniques) would undo my past and heal PTSD "once and for all." I believed that anything less than "my life is completely transformed" wasn't important. After years of working on myself, my patience for healing had also worn very thin. I wanted Tapping to heal me in six months to a year.

What I've come to understand is that while I am transforming myself and my life more deeply and wholly than ever before, there is no "magic formula" for healing. Accepting that fact has empowered me to value my mounting successes.

Tapping and especially the wisdom and Tapping meditations you offered in your course have given me a "tool kit" for processing triggering events. The gift and power of Tapping is that it works on that deep, cellular, psychic level where our emotions are rooted. Using your Tapping meditations, I've been able to feel and transform difficult feelings and misguided core beliefs. Instead of trying to intellectualize or "spiritualize" them, I now have a way—on my own and for free—to shift them.

I'm rebuilding my life with a commitment to loving and honoring myself and my art, working toward my dream in ways and at a pace that honors my needs and wants for more ease and joy.

With love and appreciation,

Lake

None of us are perfect, nor are our lives. But we grow and evolve, we rediscover our flow, and respond in new, empowering ways to old, familiar challenges. From there, we can harness our power to create positive, lasting change.

Looking Back, Moving Forward

Hindsight, as they say, is 20/20. I now know and receive daily the blessings of the Louise Hay interview that was conducted by Nick instead of me. One of those blessings, I now realize, was the months I spent alone and unwell in California. They taught me to surrender. They taught me to make a habit of finding relief. As my body healed, so did my spirit. My energy returned slowly, and with it, deep gratitude that stays with me to this day.

Thanks to my disappointment over that interview, I received the gift of Louise Hay's words, "Trust life." Without those words, I might not have had the courage to keep my heart open to the personal blessings that later unfolded. Also, Nick conducting the interview that day did, in fact, accomplish what Louise Hay intended, which was to boost the success of his first book. His success then led to my first book, a positive cycle that has expanded farther than we ever imagined possible.

Even now, the blessings born through challenging experiences continue to unfold according to their own divine timing. That's how life works. We gain trust in retrospect. We solidify our foundation *after* we expand beyond our current limitations.

Eventually we pause and notice the abundance we've realized, the courage we've gathered, and the resilience we've gained. Eventually we look around and see the bounty that our flow has allowed us to receive. Then, once again, we leap into a new unknown, calling upon our courage to evolve toward a new, more expansive vision. And with just the right touch of magic, the journey goes on.

APPENDIX

Bonus Tapping Scripts

This Appendix contains bonus scripts, some of which are extended versions of Tapping scripts referenced within this book. Others are simply extra scripts you can use if and when they resonate.

Many of the extended scripts are prefaced with a brief description from the relevant chapter. My hope is that you'll return to this Appendix as a resource to support you whenever and as often as you need it.

In the pages ahead, you'll find the following bonus Tapping scripts:

Chapter 3 Tapping Script

- Quieting a Limiting Belief

Chapter 4 Tapping Scripts

- Clearing the Fear of Taking Action
- Finding Comfort Outside Your Comfort Zone
- Enjoying the Journey toward Change

Chapter 5 Tapping Scripts

- Hoarding Scarcity
- Clearing Clutter *without* the Overwhelm
- Keeping the Memory and Letting Go of the Object

Chapter 6 Tapping Scripts

- *Drama Shrinker*—Saying No to Others So You Can Say Yes to Your Best Life
- *Drama Fixer*—Letting Go and Finding Peace
- *Drama Seeker*—Observing and Releasing Drama

Chapter 7 Tapping Scripts

- Releasing the Limiting Belief "I can't take a break if I want to succeed"
- Releasing the Limiting Belief "I have to earn self-care"
- Releasing the Limiting Belief "The more I push, the further I'll go"

Chapter 8 Tapping Scripts

- Money and Spirituality
- Clearing Financial Overwhelm

Chapter 9 Tapping Scripts

- Releasing Fear from Past Failure
- Releasing Fear of Failure
- Releasing Fear of Success—Letting Go of Limitations

Chapter 10 Tapping Scripts

- Releasing the Pressure of Perfectionism
- From Impatience to Finding Meaning and Joy

Chapter 11 Tapping Script

- Being Open to Hidden Blessings

CHAPTER 3 EXTENDED TAPPING: QUIETING A LIMITING BELIEF

Looking back at your list of negative beliefs that your critical voice says to you, pick the one belief that feels most true at this moment.

Rate how true that particular belief feels on a scale of 0 to 10, with 10 being completely true.

Take a deep breath.

We'll begin by tapping on the Karate Chop point.

Karate Chop *(repeat three times)*: Even though I've been holding on to this belief, I accept how I feel and choose to relax.

Eyebrow: This belief

Side of Eye: It feels so true

Under Eye: I've had this belief for a long time

Under Nose: <State your belief now>

Under Mouth: It's a story I keep telling myself

Collarbone: To try to protect myself from disappointment

Under Arm: Right now this feels true to me

Top of Head: And that's okay

Eyebrow: <State your belief now>

Side of Eye: It feels so true

Under Eye: This belief

Under Nose: <State your belief now>

Under Mouth: I've believed this for so long

Collarbone: This belief may not make me happy

Under Arm: But it's familiar

Top of Head: I've been holding on to this belief

Eyebrow: I like to prove that I'm right

Side of Eye: So I've been looking for evidence

Under Eye: That this limiting belief is true

Under Nose: But as I allow myself to relax

Under Mouth: Even before anything changes

Collarbone: I can take a closer look

Under Arm: I begin to doubt this belief

Top of Head: It's just a story

Eyebrow: I feel safe questioning my beliefs

Side of Eye: As I relax my mind

Under Eye: And feel centered in my body

Under Nose: I can ask myself

Under Mouth: Is this really true?

Collarbone: I don't have to believe

Under Arm: Everything I think

Top of Head: I reexamine what feels true to me

Eyebrow: I'm further along than I give myself credit for

Side of Eye: I honor my personal journey

Under Eye: And how much I've been through

Under Nose: I picked up this belief in my past

Under Mouth: But I don't need to keep it

Collarbone: I honor the emotions behind this belief

Under Arm: And practice self-compassion

Top of Head: This belief is just an old story

Eyebrow: When I feel centered and calm

Side of Eye: I can begin to connect with my truth

Under Eye: I am enough

Under Nose: Great things are possible for me

Under Mouth: And when I have doubts

Collarbone: I give myself the love and reassurance I need

Under Arm: I can relax my body now

Top of Head: I know what feels true to me

Take a deep breath. When you think about what your critical voice is saying to you, how true does it feel now? Give it a number on a scale of 0 to 10.

Keep tapping until you can have the thought without feeling anxiety or panic in any form. At that point it will no longer feel true.

CHAPTER 4 EXTENDED TAPPING: CLEARING THE FEAR OF TAKING ACTION

Faith is taking the first step even when you don't see the whole staircase.
— Martin Luther King, Jr.

Action, even imperfect action, leads us back into flow. That's because action breeds clarity. Making a course correction as we move forward *is* progress, but still we often fear the experience of taking action steps.

Let's do some Tapping on feeling safe taking action even though you don't know where that action will lead you, and even though you'll eventually face problems that you don't yet know how to solve.

To begin, rate how much fear you feel when you think about taking action when you don't know the outcome. Give it a number on a scale of 0 to 10.

Take a deep breath.

We'll begin by tapping on the Karate Chop point.

Karate Chop *(repeat three times)*: Even though I feel all this fear around taking action when I don't know how things will turn out, I honor how I feel and am open to taking a single step.

Eyebrow: All this fear

Side of Eye: I can feel it in my body

Under Eye: I want to take a step forward

Under Nose: But I feel frozen

Under Mouth: I'm unsure of what to do

Collarbone: I don't know what will work

Under Arm: I'm afraid

Top of Head: I feel stuck in place

Eyebrow: I care so much

Side of Eye: That I'm scared of making a mistake

Under Eye: It all feels overwhelming

Under Nose: I have all these questions

Under Mouth: That don't have answers yet

Collarbone: It makes me feel frozen

Under Arm: All this uncertainty

Top of Head: All this fear

Eyebrow: I keep thinking about what I should do

Side of Eye: But I'm not making progress

Under Eye: I honor my fear

Under Nose: I acknowledge all the pressure I've put on myself

Under Mouth: I want to do it perfectly

Collarbone: I want the perfect plan

Under Arm: Because this uncertainty feels so unsettling

Top of Head: I honor all these feelings

Eyebrow: And I'm open to a new approach

Side of Eye: Action breeds clarity

Under Eye: I no longer need to wait

Under Nose: I experiment with a playful spirit

Under Mouth: It's okay to be a little scared

Collarbone: And ready to take a step

Under Arm: I am navigating through something new

Top of Head: I release the pressure to know all the answers

Eyebrow: I acknowledge my fear

Side of Eye: And relax my body

Under Eye: Even without all the answers

Under Nose: I can feel centered and calm

Under Mouth: I am being guided

Collarbone: I am open to my intuition

Under Arm: It's safe to take action

Top of Head: I'm safe moving forward

Eyebrow: I do less thinking

Side of Eye: And more experimenting

Under Eye: It's safe to explore

Under Nose: I find the support around me

Under Mouth: Now is the time for action

Collarbone: I have everything I need inside of me

Under Arm: To move my dreams forward

Top of Head: It's safe to take one step forward

Take a deep breath. On a scale of 0 to 10, once again rate the intensity of your fear of creating movement even when the results are unknown. Rather than trying to tap away all of your fear, continue tapping until you simply feel willing to take action in spite of your fear. That's huge progress!

CHAPTER 4 EXTENDED TAPPING:
FINDING COMFORT OUTSIDE YOUR COMFORT ZONE

Every time we do something new and expand, every time we grow, we inevitably experience discomfort. To grow we must stretch, and stretching doesn't always feel perfect. The discomfort and fear it brings up are normal parts of the change process. They're not reasons to stop taking action or to retreat exclusively into inner work. Instead, they're a call to notice how we're feeling, to work on processing and releasing it *as* we continue creating movement in our life.

Ask yourself:

Do I tell myself that one day I'll be able to make a change, after I work on myself enough that I feel perfect? How is being stuck in my inner work serving me?

Next, notice how strongly the belief *I have to feel perfectly ready before I can find my flow* feels. Give it a number on a scale of 0 to 10.

Take a deep breath.

We'll begin by tapping on the Karate Chop point.

Karate Chop *(repeat three times)*: Even though I still have doubts, I honor how I feel and give myself permission to experiment.

Eyebrow: Part of me is ready to take action

Side of Eye: But sometimes I still have doubts

Under Eye: I'm waiting for the perfect moment

Under Nose: When I clear every doubt

Under Mouth: When I clear every insecurity

Collarbone: All this pressure I feel

Under Arm: All the self-judgment

Top of Head: I'm waiting to feel ready

Eyebrow: I've been telling myself a story

Side of Eye: That one day I'll "arrive"

Under Eye: And feel perfectly confident

Under Nose: Perfectly ready

Under Mouth: Perfectly courageous

Collarbone: I keep working on myself

Under Arm: Waiting for the perfect moment

Top of Head: When I can begin to take action

Eyebrow: I honor my desire to improve myself

Side of Eye: I honor my desire to heal

Under Eye: I acknowledge the pressure I put on myself

Under Nose: And how it's holding me back

Under Mouth: I've been so focused on what I need to fix

Collarbone: That I haven't acknowledged my gifts

Under Arm: I've been so focused on what I haven't done

Top of Head: That I haven't acknowledged how far I've come

Eyebrow: I can be really ready

Side of Eye: And still a little scared

Under Eye: I can move forward

Under Nose: Even when it feels a bit uncomfortable

Under Mouth: Everything that's new feels uncertain

Collarbone: I give myself the reassurance I need

Under Arm: It's safe to take action

Top of Head: I acknowledge my fears

Eyebrow: I honor all my feelings

Side of Eye: As I stop judging these feelings

Under Eye: It's easier to move through them

Under Nose: This is part of the process

Under Mouth: I find comfort outside my comfort zone

Collarbone: By remembering it's okay to feel the way I feel

Under Arm: I release the pressure to feel perfectly

Top of Head: I give myself the reassurance I need

Eyebrow: I honor how uncomfortable change can feel

Side of Eye: This is part of the process

Under Eye: I focus on finding more ease

Under Nose: I don't need to seek perfection

Under Mouth: I simply seek relief

Collarbone: And when I allow myself to take action

Under Arm: I discover it's easier than I thought

Top of Head: Right now and right here, I am ready

Take a deep breath. Check back in with yourself and again rate how true this belief feels on a scale of 0 to 10. Keep tapping on releasing your belief and letting yourself feel the deeper emotions behind it, such as fear of having to put yourself out there.

CHAPTER 4 EXTENDED TAPPING: ENJOYING THE JOURNEY TOWARD CHANGE

Are you delaying creating change and putting your flow on hold because of one (or several) dreams you haven't yet realized?

On a scale of 0 to 10, rate how true this statement feels: *I can't find my flow or my joy until I've* <state your goal here>.

Take a deep breath.

We'll begin by tapping on the Karate Chop point.

Karate Chop *(repeat three times)*: Even though I feel like I can't enjoy my progress until I reach my goal, I honor how I feel and I'm open to a new way.

Eyebrow: I can't feel good

Side of Eye: Until this change happens

Under Eye: I can't feel good about my progress

Under Nose: Unless I'm certain it will all work out

Under Mouth: I've been putting my joy on hold

Collarbone: I've been pushing myself

Under Arm: And feeling impatient

Top of Head: I acknowledge how hard this has been

Eyebrow: One day I'll be able to feel proud

Side of Eye: But not yet

Under Eye: One day I'll be able to feel happy

Under Nose: But not yet

Under Mouth: I've been putting my joy on hold

Collarbone: Because I've made this rule in my head

Under Arm: That I can't feel good

Top of Head: Unless I earn it

Eyebrow: Somewhere I picked up a belief

Side of Eye: That I have to earn happiness

Under Eye: Somewhere I picked up a belief

Under Nose: That I have to struggle to get what I want

Under Mouth: But this struggle is leaving me exhausted

Collarbone: And filled with worry

Under Arm: I honor how anxious I've been feeling

Top of Head: I acknowledge all of this pressure

Eyebrow: It's hard to listen to the whispers of my intuition

Side of Eye: When I don't feel calm and centered

Under Eye: It's hard to be consistent

Under Nose: When I'm not enjoying the process

Under Mouth: Maybe there is another way

Collarbone: Maybe I can make progress

Under Arm: And enjoy the process

Top of Head: I'm open to experiencing more ease

Eyebrow: Right now and right here

Side of Eye: It's safe to feel hopeful

Under Eye: Right now and right here

Under Nose: I can acknowledge how far I've come

Under Mouth: All life changes require patience

Collarbone: And it's easier to feel patient

Under Arm: When I allow myself to feel good now

Top of Head: I give myself permission to feel good now

Eyebrow: I honor every step forward

Side of Eye: I celebrate every little success

Under Eye: When I find joy within the process

Under Nose: I find my flow

Under Mouth: I can still desire more

Collarbone: And feel good about where I am

Under Arm: I can relax in this moment

Top of Head: And still dream about the future

Take a deep breath. Again, rate how true your belief that you have to realize your goal first feels on a scale of 0 to 10. Keep tapping until that belief is overshadowed by a willingness to find your flow first, before realizing that goal or dream.

CHAPTER 5 EXTENDED TAPPING: HOARDING SCARCITY

Are you struggling with letting go of items out of a scarcity mind-set? This shows up in a fear that you'll need the things in the future or a feeling that something bad could happen if you let them go.

Select an item you're struggling to let go of. Rate the intensity of your resistance to releasing it on a scale of 0 to 10.

Take a deep breath.

Begin tapping on the Karate Chop point.

Karate Chop *(repeat three times)*: Even though part of me knows it's time to let go of clutter, and another part of me holds on tightly because I'm scared of feeling more lack, I accept and honor all these feelings.

Eyebrow: Part of me knows that I'm holding on to too much

Side of Eye: I know it's time to begin to let go

Under Eye: But another part of me is scared

Under Nose: What if I regret it?

Under Mouth: What if I need it in the future?

Collarbone: Part of me wants to hold on tightly

Under Arm: Even though I'm beginning to see

Top of Head: That holding on is holding me back

Eyebrow: I've struggled with my finances

Side of Eye: I often feel a sense of lack

Under Eye: So I hold on tight to things

Under Nose: Even though these things can feel overwhelming

Under Mouth: I've been holding on tight

Collarbone: Because part of me feels that holding on will help me feel better

Under Arm: I've been doing my best

Top of Head: But I see this strategy isn't working

Eyebrow: This feeling of lack in my life

Side of Eye: I've been struggling with my finances for so long

Under Eye: Because I feel this sense of lack

Under Nose: I try to fill this void

Under Mouth By holding on to things

Collarbone: But it's only left me feeling more disempowered

Under Arm: I recognize how hard this has been

Top of Head: And I'm open to a new way

Eyebrow: Part of me knows letting go will feel good but

Side of Eye: I just want to do what I've always done

Under Eye: It's too overwhelming to let go

Under Nose: It feels too scary to let go

Under Mouth: I recognize all my resistance

Collarbone: And I honor how hard this has been

Under Arm: It's safe to acknowledge how I'm feeling

Top of Head: And I'm open to a new way of thinking

Eyebrow: Maybe this can be easier than I thought

Side of Eye: Maybe I can let go at my own pace

Under Eye: I recognize that holding on

Under Nose: Has only left me feeling overwhelmed

Under Mouth: I'm ready for abundance in my life

Collarbone: It's time to make room for abundance

Under Arm: By letting go of clutter that is weighing me down

Top of Head: It is safe to begin to let go

Eyebrow: All these things can find a new home

Side of Eye: I recognize what is useful and what makes me happy

Under Eye: And I recognize what I need to let go of.

Under Nose: I allow myself to start small

Under Mouth: And I begin to notice how good it feels to let go

Collarbone: I'm turning a new page in my life where I feel abundant

Under Arm: By recognizing how much love and light is inside of me

Top of Head: And how good it feels to let go and make room for more.

Take a deep breath. Notice how intense your resistance feels now on a scale of 0 to 10. Keep tapping until you experience the desired relief.

CHAPTER 5 EXTENDED TAPPING: CLEARING CLUTTER *WITHOUT* THE OVERWHELM

Abundance is a process of letting go; that which is empty can receive.
— Bryant H. McGill

Where do we even start when it comes to clearing clutter?

Sorting and purging our stuff feels like more chores, more work, and too many decisions. We may also feel embarrassed, even ashamed, and wonder, *How did I let it get this bad?* By tapping we can neutralize the experience, so we may not feel super excited to clear clutter at first, but we're at least willing. Once you start and notice how much better you feel, the process becomes even easier.

Let's do some Tapping on lessening that overwhelm now.

First think of a space—your home, office, car—that needs to be decluttered and notice how much overwhelm you feel when you think about doing it. Rate your overwhelm on a scale of 0 to 10.

Take a deep breath.

Begin tapping on the Karate Chop point.

Karate Chop *(repeat three times)*: Even though I feel so overwhelmed when I even think about my clutter, I accept myself and how I feel.

Eyebrow: This clutter

Side of Eye: It's so overwhelming

Under Eye: How did I let it get so bad?

Under Nose: I don't want to face it

Under Mouth: This clutter

Collarbone: It's overwhelming

Under Arm: It's too much

Top of Head: I don't want to deal with it

Eyebrow: I'm good at ignoring it

Side of Eye: Because every time I face my clutter

Under Eye: I'm faced with my own judgments

Under Nose: I feel embarrassed

Under Mouth: I feel overwhelmed

Collarbone: I feel stuck

Under Arm: I acknowledge the emotions

Top of Head: That this clutter represents

Eyebrow: I am overwhelmed by this clutter

Side of Eye: And that's okay

Under Eye: The nature of clutter is overwhelming

Under Nose: I acknowledge how hard this has been

Under Mouth: It's easier to stay the same

Collarbone: But that doesn't feel right either

Under Arm: Even though this clutter is overwhelming

Top of Head: I give myself permission to relax

Eyebrow: These things are just things

Side of Eye: I have the power to control how I feel

Under Eye: I choose to find ways to make this easier

Under Nose: By remembering that even with this clutter

Under Mouth: I'm okay

Collarbone: I'm ready to let go of what I no longer need

Under Arm: So I can make room for my true desires

Top of Head: Maybe this can be easier than I thought

Eyebrow: I imagine how good it will feel to let go

Side of Eye: As I let go of what I don't need

Under Eye: I make room for miracles

Under Nose: As I let go of what I don't need

Under Mouth: I usher in health and vitality

Collarbone: As I let go of what I don't need

Under Arm: I feel welcomed and comfortable in my own home

Top of Head: I am open to the process

Eyebrow: I release the need to do it all at once

Side of Eye: I celebrate every small step

Under Eye: All progress is worth celebrating

Under Nose: I relax into the process

Under Mouth: and find ways to make it fun

Collarbone: I move at my own pace

Under Arm: Every small step feels empowering

Top of Head: I am making room for the life of my dreams

Take a deep breath. Notice again how intense your overwhelm around clearing clutter feels, and give it a number of intensity on a scale of 0 to 10. Keep tapping until you experience the desired relief.

CHAPTER 5 EXTENDED TAPPING: KEEPING THE MEMORY AND LETTING GO OF THE OBJECT

Focus on the object you're struggling to release because of its sentimental and emotional meaning. There is nothing wrong with keeping things that have sentimental value. It becomes a problem when you're holding on to so many things that the clutter feels overwhelming, or it's taking up an overwhelming amount of space, or you pay money in storage fees every month. Whether it's time to let go of the pile of old Christmas cards you don't look at often or an heirloom you feel guilty letting go of, this Tapping can help.

Rate your resistance to letting it go on a scale of 0 to 10.

Take a deep breath.

Begin tapping on the Karate Chop point.

Karate Chop *(repeat three times)***:** Part of me wants to let go of this, and another part of me feels guilty; I honor all my feelings and remember it's safe to let go

Eyebrow: Part of me wants to let this go

Side of Eye: I know it's time to make more room in my life

Under Eye: But it has sentimental value

Under Nose: It reminds me of a special time in my life

Under Mouth: It reminds me of a special someone

Collarbone: And I feel like I'm doing something wrong

Under Arm: If I let this go

Top of Head: I recognize these conflicting feelings

Eyebrow: Part of me wants to let it go

Side of Eye: And another part of me feels guilty

Under Eye: All this guilt around letting go

Under Nose: All of this resistance

Under Mouth: I recognize the part of me that wants to hold on

Collarbone: What am I trying to hold on to?

Under Arm: Am I trying to hold on to an object

Top of Head: Or am I really trying to hold on to a memory?

Eyebrow: I've been trying to hold on to a person

Side of Eye: I've been trying to hold on to a special time in my life

Under Eye: I've been trying to hold on to a memory

Under Nose: But these memories aren't within this stuff

Under Mouth: These memories are within me

Collarbone: I hold on to the memory

Under Arm: And release the object

Top of Head: By releasing objects from the past

Eyebrow: I put my energy and attention on my future

Side of Eye: These memories are a part of who I am

Under Eye: I cherish these memories

Under Nose: These memories are not within these things

Under Mouth: These memories are within me

Collarbone: I hold on to the memories

Under Arm: And release the object

Top of Head: This object is ready for a new home

Eyebrow: I hold on to love

Side of Eye: And release this object

Under Eye: I hold on to this memory

Under Nose: And release the object

Under Mouth: My past is important to me

Collarbone: And so is my future

Under Arm: I make room for a bright future

Top of Head: By releasing what I don't truly need or want

Eyebrow: I hold on to these memories

Side of Eye: I honor my past

Under Eye: And I honor my future

Under Nose: I embrace this memory

Under Mouth: And release the object

Collarbone: It is safe to let go

Under Arm: I'm making room for more

Top of Head: Knowing that special memories always live inside of me

Take a deep breath. Notice how much resistance you feel now and rate its intensity on a scale of 0 to 10. Keep tapping until you feel the desired release.

CHAPTER 6 EXTENDED TAPPING: *DRAMA SHRINKER*—SAYING NO TO OTHERS SO YOU CAN SAY YES TO YOUR BEST LIFE

Saying no can be especially challenging for drama shrinkers, since their aim is to avoid rejection and conflict at all cost.

To begin using Tapping to establish healthy boundaries, start by thinking about a situation where you should or would like to say no. Notice any resistance or anxiety you feel, and write down those feelings.

When I think about saying no, I feel . . .

Like a disappointment

Guilty

Nervous

Like I'm not doing enough

Like I'm being selfish

Fill in others here:

_____

_____

_____

Next, rate the intensity of your primary (strongest) emotion about saying no on a scale of 0 to 10.

Next let's do some Tapping on releasing those feelings. You can replace words and phrases as needed to make your Tapping as relevant to your experience as possible.

Take a deep breath. We'll begin by tapping on the Karate Chop point.

Karate Chop (*repeat three times*): Even though I am so scared to disappoint others, I accept myself and how I feel.

Eyebrow: I can't say no

Side of Eye: They need me

Under Eye: And I can't disappoint them

Under Nose: I can't say no

Under Mouth: Just the thought of saying no

Collarbone: Creates anxiety in my body

Under Arm: All this fear

Top of Head: I just want everyone to be happy

Eyebrow: And it's exhausting

Side of Eye: And it's not working

Under Eye: I have been saying yes

Under Nose: When I want to say no

Under Mouth: I feel like I have no choice

Collarbone: And it leaves me feeling resentful

Under Arm: I acknowledge this struggle

Top of Head: I honor my resentment

Eyebrow: I'm so good at being the martyr

Side of Eye: I'd rather be unhappy than disappoint others

Under Eye: But I'm tired

Under Nose: Part of me wants to change

Under Mouth: Another part of me is scared

Collarbone: I don't like to rock the boat

Under Arm: I'd rather suffer in silence

Top of Head: But I'm exhausted

Eyebrow: I acknowledge the toll this has taken

Side of Eye: Where did I learn this belief?

Under Eye: This belief that I have to be perfect

Under Nose: And make everyone happy?

Under Mouth: I picked this up as a child

Collarbone: To keep myself safe

Under Arm: But as an adult

Top of Head: This belief isn't serving me

Eyebrow: And it isn't serving the world

Side of Eye: It's hard to share my gifts with the world

Under Eye: When I'm always sacrificing my happiness

Under Nose: Maybe I can ease into saying no

Under Mouth: Or simply say, let me get back to you

Collarbone: I give myself the time to check in

Under Arm: And see what feels right to me

Top of Head: Whether I say yes or no

Eyebrow: I am still a good person

Side of Eye: My happiness is not dependent on their approval

Under Eye: It's safe to say no to others

Under Nose: And yes to myself

Under Mouth: I choose what feels right to me

Collarbone: And I give others the permission to say no

Under Arm: I begin to practice saying no

Top of Head: So that I can say yes to myself

Take a deep breath. When you think of that same situation where you want or need to say no, how do you feel now? Rate the intensity of your primary emotion once again on a scale of 0 to 10.

Keep tapping until you can imagine saying no without experiencing any intense negative emotion.

CHAPTER 6 EXTENDED TAPPING: *DRAMA FIXER*—LETTING GO AND FINDING PEACE

If you notice yourself falling into drama fixer patterns, use Tapping to begin giving yourself the love and caring that you're seeking from others when you step into the drama fixer role.

First rate how intensely you feel the need to "fix" others' lives on a scale of 0 to 10.

Take a deep breath.

We'll start by tapping on the Karate Chop point.

Karate Chop *(repeat three times)*: Even though I feel responsible when others are having a difficult time, I love and accept myself, and I am open to a new way of thinking.

Eyebrow: I just want to help

Side of Eye: I see this drama

Under Eye: I see this person in pain

Under Nose: And I know what's right for them

Under Mouth: I know I can help

Collarbone: Part of me loves helping

Under Arm: And part of me notices a conflict

Top of Head: Because through helping everyone

Eyebrow: I have lost myself

Side of Eye: All of this worry I experience

Under Eye: All of this stress

Under Nose: I take on other people's drama

Under Mouth: Because I want to fix it

Collarbone: But I'm left tired and exhausted

Under Arm: I often sacrifice my own happiness . . .

Top of Head: In order to please others

Eyebrow: But I have always been like this

Side of Eye: People look to me to fix it

Under Eye: And I want to help

Under Nose: But I'm tired of all this worry

Under Mouth: I'm tired of the drama

Collarbone: I'm tired of the stress

Under Arm: I thought by sacrificing myself

Top of Head: I could help others

Eyebrow: But I am beginning to notice

Side of Eye: How it doesn't improve the situation

Under Eye: It just leaves me resentful

Under Nose: I can love others

Under Mouth: But it's not my job to make them happy

Collarbone: They must choose happiness for themselves

Under Arm: I can wish the best for others

Top of Head: But it's not my job to fix all their problems

Eyebrow: But part of me wants to fix all their problems

Side of Eye: Part of me likes being the drama fixer

Under Eye: This inner conflict

Under Nose: I begin to open up to the idea

Under Mouth: That I can still love someone

Collarbone: Without needing to fix them

Under Arm: I can be supportive of others

Top of Head: And create a clear boundary

Eyebrow: When I have faith that they are on their own spiritual journey

Side of Eye: I let go of trying to control and fix

Under Eye: I can love others and still say no

Under Nose: I can hope for peace and not get involved

Under Mouth: When I put my happiness first

Collarbone: I inspire others to do the same

Under Arm: When I have faith in something greater than myself . . .

Top of Head: I can let go and trust

Take a deep breath. Rate the intensity of your need to "fix" others' lives again on a scale of 0 to 10. Keep tapping until you feel more peace with the idea of relieving yourself of the responsibility of fixing others' problems.

CHAPTER 6 EXTENDED TAPPING:
DRAMA SEEKER—OBSERVING AND RELEASING DRAMA

When we're really upset about a situation, even when we're acting as a drama seeker, it can be really hard to step back and notice the role we're playing in drama. By using Tapping to process your feelings, you can feel more empowered within drama. You're then likely to act and react to situations differently.

Notice how you feel when it comes to drama and conflict in your life. Do you feel frustrated or stuck? Notice the feeling and rate the intensity on a scale of 0 to 10.

Take a deep breath.

We'll start by tapping on the Karate Chop point.

Karate Chop *(repeat three times)*: Even though I feel like drama always finds me, I honor my experience and I am open to a new way.

Eyebrow: Part of me is tired of this drama

Side of Eye: But I don't know how to end it

Under Eye: If I'm not upset, then it means I won't be heard

Under Nose: If they don't argue with me

Under Mouth: It means they don't care

Collarbone: I've been using drama to test my relationships

Under Arm: Part of me is tired of this drama

Top of Head: Part of me feels powerless to change it

Eyebrow: And part of me feels like I need it

Side of Eye: I become aware of my relationship to drama

Under Eye: I've felt like I needed to fight

Under Nose: I needed to defend myself

Under Mouth: I can't find peace

Collarbone: Until they agree with me

Under Arm: Until they fix this problem

Top of Head: All this drama

Eyebrow: All this tension

Side of Eye: I'm so used to this drama

Under Eye: I've lived with it for so long

Under Nose: Part of me hates this drama

Under Mouth: And part of me finds it exciting

Collarbone: As I allow my body to relax

Under Arm: I begin to open up to new possibilities

Top of Head: I've been focused on the problem

Eyebrow: I've been focused on what they did wrong

Side of Eye: And I haven't acknowledged how I feel

Under Eye: I take responsibility for how I feel

Under Nose: There is no battle to win

Under Mouth: There is simply something to remember

Collarbone: I am safe

Under Arm: I am enough

Top of Head: And I choose peace

Eyebrow: I begin to see what I'm truly craving

Side of Eye: I'm craving love

Under Eye: I'm craving connection

Under Nose: I want to feel heard

Under Mouth: And as I begin to give myself my own love

Collarbone: As I begin to connect with myself

Under Arm: As I begin to listen to my inner voice

Top of Head: It's easy to walk away from drama

Eyebrow: I go from focusing on the problem

Side of Eye: To focusing on the solution

Under Eye: As I honor how I feel

Under Nose: As I honor the pain behind this drama

Under Mouth: It's easy to let go of this conflict

Collarbone: As I take care of myself

Under Arm: I learn how to move past this conflict

Top of Head: I choose peace

Take a deep breath. Again, rate the intensity of the emotion you measured from 0 to 10. Keep tapping until you feel less attached to the drama and more willing to step away from it without experiencing negative emotions like fear, boredom, and so on.

CHAPTER 7 EXTENDED TAPPING: RELEASING THE LIMITING BELIEF "I CAN'T TAKE A BREAK IF I WANT TO SUCCEED"

How true does the belief *I can't take a break if I want to succeed* feel on a scale of 0 to 10? Give it a number of intensity now.

Take a deep breath.

Begin tapping on the Karate Chop point.

Karate Chop *(repeat three times)*: Even though I have this belief that I can't take a break if I want to succeed, I can relax and accept myself.

Eyebrow: This belief

Side of Eye: That I can't take a break if I want to succeed

Under Eye: It feels so true

Under Nose: Success and hard work

Under Mouth: They go hand in hand

Collarbone: Success means sacrifice

Under Arm: And that means I can't take a break

Top of Head: I have to keep going

Eyebrow: I can't make time for myself

Side of Eye: Or else I feel overwhelmed with guilt

Under Eye: I can't take a break

Under Nose: Or else I criticize myself

Under Mouth: I feel like I should be further along

Collarbone: So I keep pushing myself

Under Arm: I acknowledge how exhausted I feel

Top of Head: I acknowledge this belief

Eyebrow: That I can't take a break if I want to succeed

Side of Eye: Sometimes it feels like an uphill battle

Under Eye: And I'm unsure what to do next

Under Nose: What if always pushing isn't working?

Under Mouth: I am tired of always pushing

Collarbone: I value all my effort

Under Arm: And I'm open to valuing myself

Top of Head: By taking a break

Eyebrow: Maybe I can still work hard

Side of Eye: And find time to rest and recover

Under Eye: Maybe taking a step away

Under Nose: Will give me new perspectives and clarity

Under Mouth: This break isn't holding me back

Collarbone: It's giving me the energy I need

Under Arm: I take time to recharge my batteries

Top of Head: Self-care is essential for long-term success

Eyebrow: It's safe to take a break when I need it

Side of Eye: I may need to push sometimes

Under Eye: But then I have to rest

Under Nose: I release any old guilt

Under Mouth: Self-care is part of the process

Collarbone: It's safe for me to take a break

Under Arm: It's safe for me to relax

Top of Head: And know that taking breaks is part of my success

Eyebrow: It's safe for me to take a break

Side of Eye: It's safe for me to relax and unplug

Under Eye: I take time to connect with myself

Under Nose: So I can hear the whispers of my intuition

Under Mouth: I can succeed and still take breaks

Collarbone: It's safe for me to care for myself

Under Arm: I disconnect from the outside world

Top of Head: So that I can connect with myself

Take a deep breath. How true does the belief *I can't take a break if I want to succeed* feel now? Keep tapping until you feel the desired relief.

CHAPTER 7 EXTENDED TAPPING:
RELEASING THE LIMITING BELIEF "I HAVE TO EARN SELF-CARE"

How true does the belief *I have to earn self-care* feel on a scale of 0 to 10? Give it a number of intensity.

Take a deep breath.

Begin tapping on the Karate Chop point.

Karate Chop (*repeat three times*): Even though somewhere I've been taught that I need to earn self-care, I recognize this belief and open myself to another way of thinking.

Eyebrow: I have so much to do

Side of Eye: So many people depend on me

Under Eye: I have so many things I want to do

Under Nose: Part of me feels I should be further along by now

Under Mouth: And taking time for myself would be wrong

Collarbone: All this guilt around taking time for myself

Under Arm: All this pressure I feel to do more

Top of Head: I feel like I'm doing something wrong if I relax

Eyebrow: One day I'll experience more self-care

Side of Eye: Once everything is done

Under Eye: Once everyone is happy

Under Nose: One day I'll deserve self-care

Under Mouth: Because if I do enough

Collarbone: Maybe this guilt will go away

Under Arm: But no matter how much I do

Top of Head: I still feel some guilt taking time for myself

Eyebrow: Somewhere in my childhood I was taught

Side of Eye: That I have to earn self-care

Under Eye: That taking time for myself is selfish

Under Nose: But I'm beginning to see the consequences

Under Mouth: Of not taking time for myself

Collarbone: It's hard to hear the whispers of my intuition

Under Arm: When I'm always so busy

Top of Head: It's hard to hear my heart's desires

Eyebrow: When I don't make time for peace and quiet

Side of Eye: It's hard to navigate through life

Under Eye: When I'm not connected to myself

Under Nose: And what I truly want

Under Mouth: I'm becoming open to the idea

Collarbone: That self-care doesn't need to be earned

Under Arm: It's a necessity for living my best life

Top of Head: When I take time for myself

Eyebrow: I gain the clarity I need

Side of Eye: I recharge my batteries

Under Eye: I connect to my intuition

Under Nose: I don't need to earn self-care

Under Mouth: For it is a necessity

Collarbone: The more I take time for myself

Under Arm: The better I can show up for others

Top of Head: But even more important

Eyebrow: The more I take time for myself

Side of Eye: The more I fall in love with my own life

Under Eye: I make time for myself

Under Nose: I make room for my own life

Under Mouth: It becomes easier every time

Collarbone: It's safe to relax

Under Arm: The more I take time for myself

Top of Head: The more empowered I feel

Take a deep breath. How true does the belief *I have to earn self-care* feel now on scale of 0 to 10? Keep tapping until it no longer holds an intense emotional charge.

CHAPTER 7 EXTENDED TAPPING: RELEASING THE LIMITING BELIEF "THE MORE I PUSH, THE FURTHER I'LL GO"

How true does the belief *The more I push, the further I'll go* feel to you on a scale of 0 to 10?

Take a deep breath.

Begin tapping on the Karate Chop point.

Karate Chop (*repeat three times*): Even though I've been taught that in order to succeed, I must always push forward, I recognize the pressure and tension that comes with this belief, and I'm open to a new way of thinking

Eyebrow: Somewhere I picked up the belief

Side of Eye: That the more I push, the further I'll go

Under Eye: I was taught to sacrifice

Under Nose: And suffer in order to move forward

Under Mouth: Somewhere I picked up the belief

Collarbone: That life was meant to be hard

Under Arm: Somewhere I picked up the belief

Top of Head: That I must always push forward

Eyebrow: I recognize all these beliefs

Side of Eye: And I give myself permission to question them

Under Eye: Has the stress and pressure to push forward

Under Nose: Helped me to achieve more?

Under Mouth: Has this way of being felt sustainable?

Collarbone: My critical voice often yells at me to do more

Under Arm: It's so loud that I can't hear the whispers of my intuition

Top of Head: All this pressure to always push forward

Eyebrow: Like the ocean waves

Side of Eye: I know when it's time to move forward

Under Eye: And I know when it's time to pull back

Under Nose: No matter what stage I'm in

Under Mouth: I'm still powerful

Collarbone: Like the forest trees

Under Arm: I know when it's time to grow leaves

Top of Head: And I know when it's time to let them go

Eyebrow: Life is made up of moments of outward growth

Side of Eye: And moments of letting go

Under Eye: Each of these moments are valuable

Under Nose: It is not always the right time to push

Under Mouth: When I take time for myself

Collarbone: I can hear the whispers of my intuition

Under Arm: And I know when it's time to go

Top of Head: Or when it's time to pause

Eyebrow: I know when it's time to do more

Side of Eye: And when it's time to do less

Under Eye: Life is not about pushing

Under Nose: It's about finding my flow

Under Mouth: I move in a way that feels good

Collarbone: I've been trying to constantly push myself forward

Under Arm: I've been so hard on myself

Top of Head: I was just doing my best

Eyebrow: Now I am open to a new way

Side of Eye: It's safe to slow down

Under Eye: It's safe to pause and reflect

Under Nose: I don't need to push myself

Under Mouth: I recognize when it feels good to go

Collarbone: And when it feels good to pause

Under Arm: I honor the rhythms of my life

Top of Head: And I experience flow

Take a deep breath. How true does the belief *The more I push, the further I'll go* feel now on a scale of 0 to 10? Keep tapping until it no longer holds an emotional charge for you.

CHAPTER 8 BONUS TAPPING: MONEY AND SPIRITUALITY

How true does the belief *Making money isn't spiritual* or *Making money makes me a bad person* feel on a scale of 0 to 10? Give it a number of intensity.

Take a deep, cleansing breath.

Begin tapping on your Karate Chop point.

Karate Chop *(repeat three times)*: Even though I picked up a belief in the past that I can't be a good person and make a lot of money, I honor how I feel and I'm open to a new way of thinking.

Eyebrow: Ever since I was a child

Side of Eye: I learned beliefs about money

Under Eye: Money is the root of all evil

Under Nose: Money corrupts people

Under Mouth: Money makes you greedy

Collarbone: Money isn't spiritual

Under Arm: Making money makes you a bad person

Top of Head: I acknowledge all of these messages

Eyebrow: Even though logically I may know that's not true

Side of Eye: It often feels true

Under Eye: It's hard to manage money

Under Nose: When part of me believes it's bad

Under Mouth: It's hard to make more money

Collarbone: When a part of me is scared of it

Under Arm: No wonder I've felt blocked

Top of Head: I acknowledge all of these limited beliefs

Eyebrow: It's safe to look at my resistance to money

Side of Eye: I look at these blocks with compassion

Under Eye: And a sense of curiosity

Under Nose: Where did I pick up these beliefs?

Under Mouth: Are they really true?

Collarbone: Being poor has never helped the poor

Under Arm: Like being sick has never helped the sick

Top of Head: I've been trying to be a good person

Eyebrow: As I allow my mind and body to relax

Side of Eye: I can see that money is just money

Under Eye: It's not good or bad

Under Nose: Money is neutral

Under Mouth: Money is an exchange

Collarbone: The more value I give

Under Arm: The more money I make

Top of Head: I am in control of money

Eyebrow: And how money makes me feel

Side of Eye: I choose to give more value

Under Eye: And receive more money

Under Nose: I choose to make more money

Under Mouth: In a way that makes me feel good

Collarbone: As I organize my finances

Under Arm: And learn to feel comfortable around money

Top of Head: I can expand in other areas of my life

Eyebrow: It's safe to focus on money

Side of Eye: And learn new ways to manage and make money

Under Eye: I choose what to do with money

Under Nose: And I make it a force for good

Under Mouth: It's safe for me to make more money

Collarbone: I am open and receptive to more abundance

Under Arm: My thoughts and feelings are in harmony

Top of Head: It's safe to make money

Take a deep breath. How true does the belief *Making money isn't spiritual* or *Making money makes me a bad person* feel on a scale of 0 to 10? Keep tapping until it no longer holds an intense emotional charge.

CHAPTER 8 BONUS TAPPING:
CLEARING FINANCIAL OVERWHELM

Begin by focusing on any feelings that come up when you think about your financial situation; maybe it's panic, stress, or hopelessness. Whatever it is, notice it and measure the intensity on a scale of 0 to 10.

Take a deep breath.

Begin tapping on your Karate Chop point.

Karate Chop (*repeat three times*): Even though I feel overwhelmed when I think about my finances, I accept how I feel and I give myself permission to relax.

Eyebrow: All this stress

Side of Eye: All this worry

Under Eye: I've been struggling with my finances

Under Nose: I try hard to make it better

Under Mouth: But it often feels hopeless

Collarbone: All this financial stress

Under Arm: I notice how it feels in my body

Top of Head: I notice my own thoughts

Eyebrow: I've lived with this stress for a long time

Side of Eye: Part of me believes I have to

Under Eye: It would be irresponsible not to worry

Under Nose: Because things need to change

Under Mouth: I depend on this stress

Collarbone: To push me forward

Under Arm: If I don't panic

Top of Head: It means I don't care

Eyebrow: Is that really true?

Side of Eye: I can't release this stress

Under Eye: Until my problem is solved

Under Nose: But it's hard to think clearly

Under Mouth: When I feel overwhelmed

Collarbone: I honor how I feel

Under Arm: I've been doing the best I can

Top of Head: I am open to a new way

Eyebrow: I begin to let go of all these judgments

Side of Eye: That I have around my financial situation

Under Eye: I allow my body to relax

Under Nose: Because even in my current financial situation

Under Mouth: I can feel calm and centered

Collarbone: It's safe to release this overwhelm

Under Arm: Because I am in control

Top of Head: I am present with my body

Eyebrow: As I address my fears

Side of Eye: I take my power back

Under Eye: Deep down I know things are changing

Under Nose: Deep down I know I am capable of making money

Under Mouth: In a way that feels good

Collarbone: I can look at my situation from a place of compassion

Under Arm: I am okay where I am

Top of Head: And I know things are getting better

Eyebrow: I am clear and focused

Side of Eye: I can ask for support

Under Eye: As I manage my emotions

Under Nose: I can better manage my money

Under Mouth: I look at my financial situation

Collarbone: From a place of love and compassion

Under Arm: I am in control

Top of Head: I am calm and open to solutions

Eyebrow: This past experience is a building block

Side of Eye: To a brighter future

Under Eye: Whether things go as planned or not

Under Nose: I have my own back

Under Mouth: It's safe to try

Collarbone: It's safe to experiment

Under Arm: I honor all the lessons I've learned from my past

Top of Head: I feel safe moving forward

Take a deep breath. Again rate how intensely you feel that past failure on a scale of 0 to 10. Keep tapping until you can recall the event and experience with much less negative emotional charge.

CHAPTER 9 EXTENDED TAPPING: RELEASING FEAR FROM PAST FAILURE

First, notice how intensely you experience feelings of failure when you focus on that event or part of your life. Rate their intensity on a scale of 0 to 10.

Take a deep breath.

Begin tapping on the Karate Chop point.

Karate Chop (*repeat three times*): Even though I remember a time in my past when I failed, and I'm so disappointed, I deeply and completely accept myself.

Eyebrow: I can remember a time in my past

Side of Eye: When I really tried

Under Eye: And I was left disappointed

Under Nose: I felt like I failed

Under Mouth: I remember how I felt in that moment

Collarbone: I remember how I felt judged

Under Arm: I felt humiliated

Top of Head: I felt embarrassed

Eyebrow: When I think of that past event

Side of Eye: I notice how I feel in my body

Under Eye: I honor the emotions that come up

Under Nose: It was a difficult time

Under Mouth: I'm so scared of reliving that experience

Collarbone: So I don't want to put myself out there

Under Arm: But I'm already reliving the experience

Top of Head: Every time I think about it

In as much detail as possible, retell the story of that past failure while continuing to tap through the points. When you are ready, tap through the following Tapping rounds:

Eyebrow: I honor how hard that moment was for me

Side of Eye: I was doing the best I could

Under Eye: Now that I know better

Under Nose: I can do better

Under Mouth: I've been fearing pain that's already happened

Collarbone: I take what I learned

Under Arm: And release the pain

Top of Head: That event has led me to this moment

Eyebrow: Where I honor my courage

Side of Eye: Even though that experience happened

Under Eye: I can feel calm and centered now

Under Nose: Even though that experience happened

Under Mouth: I am okay and safe

Collarbone: I've lived through so much already

Under Arm: I am resilient

Top of Head: I am stronger than I give myself credit for

Eyebrow: This past experience is a building block

Side of Eye: To a brighter future

Under Eye: Whether things go as planned or not

Under Nose: I have my own back

Under Mouth: It's safe to try

Collarbone: It's safe to experiment

Under Arm: I honor all the lessons I've learned from my past

Top of Head: I feel safe moving forward

Take a deep breath. Again rate how intensely you feel that past failure on a scale of 0 to 10. Keep tapping until you can recall the event and experience with much less negative emotional charge.

CHAPTER 9 EXTENDED TAPPING: RELEASING FEAR OF FAILURE

If you will be irritated by every rub, how will you be polished?

— Rumi

Too often we create a big story around what will happen if we try something and fail. When we use Tapping to release its negative emotional charge, we are no longer stuck in fear. Instead, we can trust in our dreams and take positive action toward them.

With Tapping our goal is to change the way we react to disappointment, not to never feel disappointed again.

Focus on something that you would like to do or make or have happen in your future. When you think about it, ask yourself, *What story do I tell myself about what will happen if I try and fail?*

Next ask yourself, *How is procrastination keeping me safe? Is it allowing me to avoid failure? Is it protecting me from the disappointment I feel when I fail? Is it protecting me from the harsh way I treat myself when I make a mistake?*

Tune in to your feelings surrounding the possibility of trying something and failing, and rate their intensity on a scale of 0 to 10.

Take a deep, cleansing breath.

Begin tapping on the Karate Chop point.

Karate Chop (*repeat three times*): Even though I'm scared to try, I honor how I feel, and I give myself permission to relax.

Eyebrow: I'm scared to try

Side of Eye: What if I fail?

Under Eye: What if I disappoint others?

Under Nose: What if I disappoint myself?

Under Mouth: I can't try

Collarbone: I might fail

Under Arm: And that's way too risky

Top of Head: It's better to not try at all

Eyebrow: It's easier for me to stay where I am

Side of Eye: I'm not happy

Under Eye: But I'm comfortable

Under Nose: I want more

Under Mouth: But I'm scared of the cost

Collarbone: I'm scared of the unknown

Under Arm: Part of me wants to stay where I am

Top of Head: And part of me wants to take a step forward

Eyebrow: I've created a story in my mind

Side of Eye: That if things don't go as planned

Under Eye: I won't be able to bear the disappointment

Under Nose: I've created a story in my mind

Under Mouth: That it's safer to just think about my dream

Collarbone: Rather than take action

Under Arm: Because things may not go as planned

Top of Head: This fear has left me stuck

Eyebrow: I acknowledge how I feel

Side of Eye: And I'm open to looking at this in a new way

Under Eye: Failure isn't the opposite of success

Under Nose: It's part of it

Under Mouth: By giving myself the freedom to try

Collarbone: And make mistakes

Under Arm: I'll find my path

Top of Head: I allow myself to experiment

Eyebrow: I've been scared of taking action

Side of Eye: Because it might not go as planned

Under Eye: But no great story has ever gone as planned

Under Nose: I am open to an adventure

Under Mouth: I'm open to making this fun

Collarbone: And if I face disappointment

Under Arm: It becomes one chapter of my greater story

Top of Head: I've been telling myself an old story

Eyebrow: That if I try and fail

Side of Eye: Then it means I'm not good enough

Under Eye: I notice this irrational fear and belief

Under Nose: And I replace it with reassurance

Under Mouth: No matter what happens

Collarbone: I'll eventually find my way

Under Arm: No matter what happens

Top of Head: I'll be okay

Take a deep breath. Again rate the intensity of your fear of future failure on a scale of 0 to 10. Keep tapping until you feel the desired relief.

CHAPTER 9 EXTENDED TAPPING:
RELEASING FEAR OF SUCCESS—LETTING GO OF LIMITATIONS

To begin lessening fear around success, let's first do some general Tapping on it.

Rate how afraid you feel when you envision achieving success in whatever way or part of your life where you most desire it. Focus on what that success will feel like. Then ask yourself, *What will I have to give up to experience that success? What feels uncomfortable and unsafe about realizing this kind of success?*

On a scale of 0 to 10, how afraid are you of achieving and maintaining that success, or of suffering from any negative consequences you envision coming from that success?

Take a deep, cleansing breath.

We'll begin by tapping on your Karate Chop point.

Karate Chop (*repeat three times*): Even though part of me wants to succeed and another part of me is scared of what that will mean, I acknowledge and accept all parts of me.

Eyebrow: I have a dream

Side of Eye: I have a desire

Under Eye: And part of me is really ready

Under Nose: And another part of me is scared

Under Mouth: I'm scared of the downside

Collarbone: What if I can't keep up with expectations?

Under Arm: What if others are jealous?

Top of Head: What if it's not sustainable?

Eyebrow: I acknowledge my doubts

Side of Eye: What is the downside of getting what I want?

Under Eye: It's safe to acknowledge my fear

Under Nose: It's been controlling my actions

Under Mouth: Sometimes I feel like I'm taking one step forward

Collarbone: And two steps back

Under Arm: I acknowledge that I've been holding myself back

Top of Head: I replace criticism with curiosity

Eyebrow: Somewhere in my past I learned

Side of Eye: That it wasn't safe to shine

Under Eye: I learned not to take up too much space

Under Nose: I was just trying to protect myself

Under Mouth: I was doing the best I could

Collarbone: But that strategy is no longer serving me

Under Arm: Part of me wants to keep playing small

Top of Head: Because it feels safe and familiar

Eyebrow: Another part of me is ready to shine

Side of Eye: I am older and wiser now

Under Eye: I am in control

Under Nose: I can navigate through a new experience

Under Mouth: I have the power to change my mind

Collarbone: I can say no when I need to say no

Under Arm: And yes when I want to say yes

Top of Head: I choose to feel centered and calm

Eyebrow: I can care about what everyone else thinks

Side of Eye: At the expense of my happiness

Under Eye: Or I can care what I think

Under Nose: And shine brightly

Under Mouth: What I think matters

Collarbone: And I have much to share with others

Under Arm: I am free to be me

Top of Head: Free to experiment

Eyebrow: Free to find my own way

Side of Eye: I have courage and faith

Under Eye: It's safe to shine

Under Nose: Because no matter what happens

Under Mouth: I have my own back

Collarbone: As I shine my light

Under Arm: I give others permission to do the same

Top of Head: It's safe to succeed

Take a deep breath. Rate how intense your fear of success feels now on a scale of 0 to 10. Keep tapping until you experience the desired relief.

CHAPTER 10 EXTENDED TAPPING: RELEASING THE PRESSURE OF PERFECTIONISM

An unhealthy fear of criticism often comes from an unhealed event in the past that caused us pain. Hoping to avoid feeling that pain again, we resolve to work hard at being perfect. Since perfection is unattainable, however, we end up causing ourselves additional pain.

Once we address the original pain that is pushing us toward perfectionism, we realize criticism can't really harm us. That's when we can form a healthier relationship with self-criticism and begin to release the belief that we need to be perfect. In that process we regain the freedom to consistently try new things and experiment, instead of being restricted by fear of making mistakes. Let's do some general Tapping to pinpoint an event that contributed to your perfectionism.

When you think of the statement *I must be perfect to avoid criticism*, how true does that feel, from 0 to 10?

Take a deep breath.

Begin by tapping on the Karate Chop point.

Karate Chop (*repeat three times*): Even though I learned as a child that I must be perfect in order to avoid being criticized, I honor my experience and accept myself.

Eyebrow: Somewhere in my past

Side of Eye: I picked up the idea

Under Eye: That I must be perfect

Under Nose: In order to deserve love

Under Mouth: Somewhere in my past

Collarbone: I picked up the idea

Under Arm: That I must be perfect

Top of Head: In order to avoid being criticized

Eyebrow: So nothing is worth doing

Side of Eye: If I can't do it perfectly

Under Eye: I quit before I finish

Under Nose: Because if I can't do it perfectly

Under Mouth: It's not worth doing

Collarbone: I'm so scared of not doing something well enough

Under Arm: Because it reminds me of pain in the past

Top of Head: Where I picked up a belief that I must be perfect

Eyebrow: In order to deserve love

Side of Eye: This perfectionism was me trying to protect myself

Under Eye: Protecting myself from pain

Under Nose: Protecting myself from disappointments

Under Mouth: But this habit of perfectionism

Collarbone: Has left me feeling stuck and disappointed

Under Arm: All these years I've just been trying to protect myself

Top of Head: From the pain I experienced in the past

Take a deep breath. After doing a few rounds of Tapping, pause and reflect.

Was there an event in the past where you learned you had to be perfect in order to be loved? Was there an event where you were criticized, and you vowed to be perfect in order to avoid that pain?

If an event comes to mind, before moving on with this Tapping script, take some time to tap on your own, using words to describe what happened and how you felt (sadness, shame, anger, and so on).

Note: If the event feels too painful, pretend that event is a movie. Give that movie a title—it can be as simple as *That Time I Was Humiliated*—and tap while simply saying that movie title until you feel more at ease with moving forward with more specifics.

If a particular event doesn't come up, that's okay too. Spend some time tapping on the fears that you currently feel, and then continue tapping through the rest of the meditation when you are ready.

Eyebrow: All this time I was just trying to protect myself

Side of Eye: I wasn't following through on things

Under Eye: For a fear that it wouldn't be perfect

Under Nose: Fear that imperfection would cause me pain

Under Mouth: I was doing the best I could

Collarbone: I was just trying to protect myself

Under Arm: As I see this pattern clearly

Top of Head: I experience deep compassion for myself

Eyebrow: I don't want to be criticized

Side of Eye: But if I am, I'll be okay

Under Eye: Even if I make a mistake

Under Nose: I deserve my own love

Under Mouth: I will no longer abandon myself

Collarbone: I will no longer abandon a dream

Under Arm: When something doesn't go perfectly

Top of Head: As I release this fear of being criticized

Eyebrow: And this desire to be perfect

Side of Eye: I feel a sense of freedom

Under Eye: I can try new things

Under Nose: I can experiment

Under Mouth: I can persevere

Collarbone: I can be consistent

Under Arm: Without the burden of perfection

Top of Head: I'm free to be me

Take a deep breath. Check in with how you feel. How true does that old belief that you have to be perfect feel, from 0 to 10? Continue tapping until you feel the desired relief.

CHAPTER 10 EXTENDED TAPPING: FROM IMPATIENCE TO FINDING MEANING AND JOY

If it's not pleasurable, it's not sustainable.

When we assign meaning to the process of being consistent in any part of our lives, we transform something we've dreaded into a source of mental, emotional, and physical nourishment. We add ease and flow to the experience of taking consistent action.

Whatever task or part of your life where you're seeking more consistency, try adding more meaning and joy to the process.

Let's do some Tapping on feeling centered where you are now.

First notice, when you think about taking consistent action, how intensely resistant—impatient, dissatisfied, frustrated, and the like—you feel on a scale of 0 to 10.

Take a deep breath and begin tapping.

Karate Chop *(repeat three times)*: Even though I'm feeling really unsure and impatient with where I am, I honor how I feel and choose to relax.

Eyebrow: I'm not where I should be

Side of Eye: It doesn't feel good

Under Eye: It feels like I'll never get where I want to be

Under Nose: Feeling impatient and unsure

Under Mouth: Not happy with where I am now

Collarbone: I should be farther along

Under Arm: All this impatience

Top of Head: It's stealing my joy

Eyebrow: I'm so focused on the end result

Side of Eye: That I'm suffering through the process

Under Eye: I feel impatient

Under Nose: I feel like I'm working hard

Under Mouth: But things aren't changing fast enough

Collarbone: Is it even worth it?

Under Arm: I acknowledge all the doubts that arise

Top of Head: When change doesn't happen as quickly as I'd like it to

Eyebrow: I acknowledge my frustration

Side of Eye: And my impatience

Under Eye: Part of me believes I can't be happy

Under Nose: Until I begin to see the fruit of my labor

Under Mouth: I've planted a seed

Collarbone: But it's not sprouting quickly enough

Under Arm: I can choose to suffer as I wait

Top of Head: Or find peace

Eyebrow: Maybe everything is unfolding as it should

Side of Eye: I trust that things are lining up

Under Eye: I could quit now

Under Nose: Or move forward with trust

Under Mouth: Every person I look up to

Collarbone: Has faced moments of doubt and impatience

Under Arm: Maybe this moment

Top of Head: Is part of a greater story

Eyebrow: Maybe I can find moments of joy

Side of Eye: Even before I see the fruits of my labor

Under Eye: Every step forward

Under Nose: Is confirmation that I am ready

Under Mouth: Every time I relax and trust

Collarbone: I can better hear my intuition

Under Arm: Even before anything changes

Top of Head: I can feel proud of myself

Eyebrow: This moment will make a great story one day

Side of Eye: This moment is enriching my life

Under Eye: As I find more joy in the process

Under Nose: I find it easier to stay the course

Under Mouth: I give myself permission to feel good now

Collarbone: Even before anything changes

Under Arm: I know this is a chapter

Top of Head: Of a greater story

Take a deep breath. Rate your impatience again on a scale of 0 to 10. Keep tapping until you feel the desired level of peace.

CHAPTER 11 EXTENDED TAPPING: BEING OPEN TO HIDDEN BLESSINGS

Be very honest with yourself. When you think about a difficult change you're experiencing, do you feel hopeful that there will be a hidden blessing behind the change? Do you have faith that good will come? On a scale of 0 to 10, how open do you feel to being patient and having faith a blessing will appear?

Take a deep breath.

Begin by tapping on the Karate Chop point.

Karate Chop (*repeat three times*): Even though I'm going through a difficult time in my life, I accept how I feel and I'm open to the idea that good will come.

Eyebrow: Things aren't going as planned

Side of Eye: So much is changing

Under Eye: And it's not the kind of change I wanted

Under Nose: I often feel powerless

Under Mouth: So much is going on

Collarbone: That feels outside of my control

Under Arm: I'm going through a difficult time

Top of Head: I'm faced with a difficult situation

Eyebrow: I honor how difficult this has been

Side of Eye: I recognize how disappointed I feel

Under Eye: Right now it doesn't feel right

Under Nose: It doesn't feel fair

Under Mouth: I acknowledge how I feel

Collarbone: This change has been hard to handle

Under Arm: Because it's not what I want

Top of Head: I honor how I feel

Eyebrow: I focus on this moment

Side of Eye: Right now and right here

Under Eye: I'm okay

Under Nose: Right now and right here

Under Mouth: I can relax my body

Collarbone: Right now and right here

Under Arm: I can breathe deeply

Top of Head: As I feel centered and calm

Eyebrow: It's easier for me to remember

Side of Eye: All I've been through

Under Eye: I've been disappointed before

Under Nose: And have found my way

Under Mouth: This experience may feel difficult

Collarbone: But it's enriching my soul

Under Arm: This moment is a catalyst for growth

Top of Head: Life has more depth and meaning

Eyebrow: After you've weathered the storm

Side of Eye: And no storm lasts forever

Under Eye: I have faith that the sun will appear

Under Nose: I have faith that from this experience

Under Mouth: Good will come

Collarbone: I am open to seeing the hidden blessings

Under Arm: As they slowly reveal themselves

Top of Head: I may not see them now

Eyebrow: But I have faith

Side of Eye: One day this moment will be part

Under Eye: Of a greater story

Under Nose: And I will see clearly

Under Mouth: How change was happening

Collarbone: For my greater good

Under Arm: From the darkness

Top of Head: I will discover my own light

Take a deep breath. Again rate how intensely you feel like this change has happened to you on a scale of 0 to 10. Keep tapping until you feel the desired release.

ENDNOTES

Tapping Quick Start Guide

1. "EFT Changes Your Genes," EFTUniverse.com. http://www.eftuniverse.com/index.php?option=com_acymailing&ctrl=archive&task=view&mailid=1014&key=Ci074lpL&tmpl=component.

Chapter 1

1. Rick Hanson, Ph.D., *Hardwiring Happiness* (New York: Harmony Books, 2013), 19–21.
2. Ibid.

Chapter 6

1. "Why We Care about What Other People Think of Us," *Psychology Today*, December 31, 2014. https://www.psychologytoday.com/blog/enlightened-living/201412/why-we-care-about-what-other-people-think-us.

Chapter 7

1. "Association between Social Media Use and Depression among U.S. Young Adults," *Depression and Anxiety* 33(4): 323–331. DOI: 10.1002/da.22466.

Chapter 8

1. Mike Dooley, "Letting Go of the Cursed Hows and Moving with Your Dreams," TUT.com, December 3, 2014. http://www.tut.com/article/details/15-letting-go-of-the-cursed-hows-and-moving-with-your-dreams/?articleId=15

INDEX

Note: Page numbers in *italics* indicate bonus/complete Tapping scripts.

E

F

ACKNOWLEDGMENTS

Writing a book is a continual practice of getting unstuck and finding your flow. In addition to Tapping throughout the journey (of course!), I can't complete this process without acknowledging the generosity of those who allowed me to share their experiences and breakthroughs. Your stories helped bring this book to life and I am so grateful.

To my husband, Lucas, so much of this book was inspired by the journey I was on right before meeting you. Every step was worthwhile because it led me to you. I love you and cherish this adventure we are on.

To my brothers, Nick and Alex, when I was five years old you stuck me inside a laundry basket, threw a towel over my head and pushed me down the stairs. As I sped down, I screamed with a mixture of fear and delight. In one brief moment the towel moved enough for me to notice that neither of you had fully let go. You each held to an edge of the basket and raced down with me. That sums us up. You both push me to be brave, you tease me, and you always guide me (at least enough to prevent any major crashes!). None of this would be possible without you. I am forever grateful.

To my mom and dad, from a young age you showed me the power of empathy, love, vulnerability, and courage. Seeing you become grandparents has been such a joy. I love you both so much and am so thankful for all your support.

I grew up reading books published by Hay House and it's a dream to be part of this family. Thank you, Reid Tracy, for being a wonderful mentor and friend.

Thank you, Patty Gift, for your support, guidance, and friendship. I will always cherish the memories of our days in Paris. Anne, thank you for your patience and encouragement to make this book the best it can be.

Thank you, Deanna Maree, for making this book beautiful with your art. You live on the other side of the world, but fate connected us.

To Wyndham, working together is a joy and I am forever grateful.

To Cheryl Richardson, good thing you've already written so many amazing books or else I'd have to write a book simply filled with the brilliant wisdom you have shared with me. You are a mentor and generous friend. Thank you.

Thank you to The Tapping Solution team. You make this dream possible. A special thank-you to Julie for your patience and incredible talent in creating the cover and Lori and Kelly for your dedication and love.

And lastly, I sprinkle an abundance of gratitude on Malakai, Lucas, Olivia, June, Karen, Brenna, my incredible family in Argentina, Maria Rosa, Javier, Ro, Eli, Sabri, Maxi, and Sebi, as well as Deirdre, Sarah, Erin, Shonda, Alex, Bex, Sam, and so, so many more. My life is blessed because of the people I have around me.

ABOUT THE AUTHOR

Jessica Ortner is the *New York Times* best-selling author of *The Tapping Solution for Weight Loss & Body Confidence* and co-producer of *The Tapping Solution* documentary film about EFT Tapping.

Jessica has led more than 10,000 women through her revolutionary Weight Loss and Body Confidence online program. She also hosts her *Adventures in Happiness* podcast, as well as The Tapping Solution *Bits and Pieces* podcast. Together, they have been downloaded more than a million times.

In partnership with her brothers Nick and Alex, Jessica has helped to create The Tapping Solution, a company on a mission to bring the simple, effective natural healing power of EFT Tapping into the mainstream. The Tapping Solution has been featured in *Women's Health*, *Psychology Today*, and *Prevention* and on *TODAY*.

Jessica currently lives in Sandy Hook, Connecticut, with her husband, Lucas.

Follow Jessica on Twitter @JessicaOrtner and on Facebook at facebook.com/followingJessicaOrtner.

Website: thetappingsolution.com

Hay House Titles of Related Interest

YOU CAN HEAL YOUR LIFE, the movie, starring Louise Hay & Friends
(available as a 1-DVD program, an expanded 2-DVD set,
and an online streaming video)
Learn more at www.hayhouse.com/louise-movie

THE SHIFT, the movie,
starring Dr. Wayne W. Dyer
(available as a 1-DVD program, an expanded 2-DVD set,
and an online streaming video)
Learn more at www.hayhouse.com/the-shift-movie

***

THE TAPPING SOLUTION: A Revolutionary System for Stress-Free Living, by Nick Ortner

THE TAPPING SOLUTION FOR MANIFESTING YOUR GREATEST SELF:
21 Days to Releasing Self-Doubt, Cultivating Inner Peace, and Creating a Life You Love,
by Nick Ortner

EVERYTHING IS HERE TO HELP YOU: A Loving Guide to Your Soul's Evolution,
by Matt Kahn

MAKING LIFE EASY: A Simple Guide to a Divinely Inspired Life,
by Christiane Northrup, M.D.

THE SACRED 6: The Simple Step-by-Step Process for Focusing Your Attention
& Recovering Your Dreams, by JB Glossinger

All of the above are available at your local bookstore,
or may be ordered by contacting Hay House (see next page).

***

We hope you enjoyed this Hay House book. If you'd like to receive
our online catalog featuring additional information on Hay House
books and products, or if you'd like to find out more about the
Hay Foundation, please contact:

Hay House, Inc., P.O. Box 5100, Carlsbad, CA 92018-5100
(760) 431-7695 or (800) 654-5126
(760) 431-6948 (fax) or (800) 650-5115 (fax)
www.hayhouse.com® • www.hayfoundation.org

———

Published in Australia by:
Hay House Australia Pty. Ltd., 18/36 Ralph St., Alexandria NSW 2015
Phone: 612-9669-4299 • *Fax:* 612-9669-4144 • www.hayhouse.com.au

Published in the United Kingdom by:
Hay House UK, Ltd., Astley House, 33 Notting Hill Gate, London W11 3JQ
Phone: 44-20-3675-2450 • *Fax:* 44-20-3675-2451 • www.hayhouse.co.uk

Published in India by: Hay House Publishers India,
Muskaan Complex, Plot No. 3, B-2, Vasant Kunj, New Delhi 110 070
Phone: 91-11-4176-1620 • *Fax:* 91-11-4176-1630 • www.hayhouse.co.in

———

<u>Access New Knowledge.</u>
<u>Anytime. Anywhere.</u>

Learn and evolve at your own pace
with the world's leading experts.

www.hayhouseU.com

Free e-newsletters
from Hay House, the Ultimate
Resource for Inspiration

Be the first to know about Hay House's free downloads, special offers, giveaways, contests, and more!

 Get exclusive excerpts from our latest releases and videos from *Hay House Present Moments*.

 Our *Digital Products Newsletter* is the perfect way to stay up-to-date on our latest discounted eBooks, featured mobile apps, and Live Online and On Demand events.

 Learn with real benefits! *HayHouseU.com* is your source for the most innovative online courses from the world's leading personal growth experts. Be the first to know about new online courses and to receive exclusive discounts.

 Enjoy uplifting personal stories, how-to articles, and healing advice, along with videos and empowering quotes, within *Heal Your Life*.

 Have an inspirational story to tell and a passion for writing? Sharpen your writing skills with insider tips from *Your Writing Life*.

Sign Up Now!

Get inspired, educate yourself, get a complimentary gift, and share the wisdom!

Visit www.hayhouse.com/newsletters to sign up today!